Letters to My Weird Sisters

Also by Joanne Limburg

NONFICTION:

Small Pieces: A Book of Lamentations
The Woman Who Thought Too Much: A Memoir of Obsession and Compulsion

FICTION:

A Want of Kindness: a novel of Queen Anne

POETRY COLLECTIONS:

The Autistic Alice
Paraphernalia
Femenismo

Letters to My Weird Sisters

Joanne Limburg

Atlantic Books
London

First published in hardback in Great Britain in 2021 by Atlantic Books,
an imprint of Atlantic Books Ltd.

10 9 8 7 6 5

A CIP catalogue record for this book is available from the British Library.

Hardback ISBN: 978 1 83895 005 7
Ebook ISBN: 978 1 83895 006 4

Printed in Great Britain by TJ Books Ltd, Padstow, Cornwall

Atlantic Books
An imprint of Atlantic Books Ltd
Ormond House
26–27 Boswell Street
London WC1N 3JZ

www.atlantic-books.co.uk

MIX
Paper from
responsible sources
FSC® C013056

i.m.

Caron Freeborn

1966–2020

Contents

Foreword:

Letter to the Reader, from Uncanny Valley

Dear Reader

You may have heard of Uncanny Valley. It's the term game designers, animators and animatronic designers use to refer to the uncomfortable feeling you get when you encounter a representation of a human figure that isn't quite human enough to convince, but is at the same time so very nearly human that the resemblance seems to call the lines between human/not-human and fake/real into question.

For some reason, human beings set a lot of store by the distinction between ourselves and everything else that exists, and it makes us uncomfortable when we can't locate it clearly. We call that feeling of discomfort – of something's being subtly, but indescribably 'off' – the feeling of uncanniness, from the German *Unheimlichkeit*, which literally means 'unhomelike', unsettled. We prefer a thing to be either familiar or strange, so that we know whether to welcome it or treat it with suspicion. When we're faced with the strangely familiar, we don't know how we're supposed to react.

Freud didn't formulate the concept of the uncanny – that was the German psychiatrist Ernst Jentsch – but he explored it in some detail in one of his best-known papers, where he defined it as an 'aesthetic experience', the subjective impression belonging to the person who encounters the unsettling object.[1] You can read work on this experience of uncanniness in all kinds of journals on all kinds of subjects. You'll probably have come across it, for example, in connection with ghost stories or horror films or photography. We know a lot about how it feels to encounter The Uncanny. We don't talk so much about how it feels to embody it, but it does happen.

I'm pretty sure that everyone, at some time, has the experience of being uncanny. I'm also fairly sure that, for most people, their experiences are rare, fleeting one-offs: maybe you met a distant relative at a family event and they thought for a moment that they were looking at your parent at the same age; maybe you were drunk or otherwise intoxicated in a way that made other people uneasy around you; maybe you found yourself briefly among strangers who didn't have a way of reading you; maybe you simply appeared for a moment at a time and in a place where the appearance of a person of your type was entirely unexpected. Think of the look you get from a room full of people when you open a door by mistake, and they're in the middle of something – a meeting, a seminar, a formal do with speeches – that frozen look that's a mixture of shock and blankness with a hint of hostility. When you encounter it, you freeze in turn. Your stomach drops. You mutter an apology and close the door. I know that look very well and I don't even have to stumble into the wrong room to get it. I can elicit it just by walking down the street.

For my particular place and time, there's nothing obviously other about me. I'm a middle-aged white woman in a majority-white country. I'm not tall and I'm only ordinarily short. I dress like you'd expect a middle-aged straight white cis-woman to dress. I'm on legs rather than wheels, and I can use them without a stick, or cane, or any other kind of mobility aid. I'm not unusually fat or thin. My person and face aren't remarkable either for their conventional attractiveness or for their distance from it. I don't have a guide dog or a white stick. I wear glasses, but so do a lot of people. If anything, I'm remarkably nondescript. (If you want more convincing, a journalist once wrote that I was small, slight, bespectacled, nervous-looking and mousy-haired. I am not, nor have I ever been, mousy-haired – I can only attribute this mistake to an overwhelming perception of general mousiness. You see – nondescript.)

I don't startle people as much as I used to, partly because I've learned how to arrange my face for the outside world, and also partly because I've reached the age of female invisibility. It still happens sometimes, though, usually when I'm particularly tired or stressed or preoccupied, and it happens like this: I'll be walking down the street, I'll catch someone's eye incidentally, and their facial expression will change, not in a good way. A smile will disappear, a neutral look turn to one of bewilderment or anxiety; if we've reached that point when two strangers approach each other on a pavement, and it's time to do the avoidance dance, they'll step aside a beat too soon; sometimes, for no reason that I can see, they'll apologize.

'Ah,' you're thinking, 'Resting Bitch Face.' It is that, but it's more than that, and other people's problematic reactions to my presence don't begin and end on the street. All my life, in all kinds of contexts, I've watched people sense something other about me, and react accordingly: some people back away as soon as they can, or push me away; some people narrow their eyes and try to figure me out; some read it as vulnerability and become protective; others read it as vulnerability and become predatory;

a few people are drawn to it. One of my infant school teachers ordered me to smile; one of my junior school teachers told me 'not to look like that'. People tell me I look furious when I'm simply trying to concentrate. People start conversations I wasn't expecting and then tell me not to look so scared. People have told me I'm too fidgety; other people have said that I'm so still it freaks them out. Oh, and apparently I have a 'distinctive walk'. My voice is too quiet but also too loud. And what am I looking at all the way over there?

I unsettle people. I'm uncanny. Being around me doesn't always feel like being around a fellow human being, and that discomfort rarely brings out the best in people. If you don't register someone as a fellow human being, you are less inclined to treat them like one. They're a threat or a nuisance or an instrument or an object or your work or your responsibility or an interesting spectacle, but not a person. It's horrible being a not-person – people who know themselves to be people will stand right in front of you, and talk about you in the third person as if you weren't even there. You'll try and get their attention and they'll act like no one spoke. It's social death.

I'm not claiming that it's a rare experience, being dehumanized; you don't have to be uncanny for it to happen. On the contrary, I'm sure most of you will have been on the receiving end of it at some point. As a matter of routine, adults do it to children; men do it to women; bosses do it to subordinates; white people do it to people of colour; abled people do it to disabled people; high status people do it to the people who serve them and clean up after them; medical staff do it to patients; anyone who walks past a homeless person on the street and doesn't acknowledge them has done it. If you're a white, middle-class, heterosexual, able-bodied cis-male, it won't have happened to you so much. If you're a black, working-class, queer, disabled, trans-female, then I'm aware that it will have happened to you a great deal more than it's happened to me.

But it has happened to me more than you might expect, and it's happened mostly because I'm uncanny, or weird, or, since my very late diagnosis, autistic.

At this point, you'll be expecting a definition of autism, and the usual way of meeting this expectation would be to look it up in a diagnostic manual – the *DSM-5*, say – or from some other official source: an institute, a research centre, the NHS, the National Autistic Society. I'm not going to do that. First of all, you can very easily do it yourselves, and if you're interested enough to pick this book up, you probably already have. Secondly, I wouldn't want to mislead you into thinking that there is any general agreement as to what autism is – there really, really isn't. Thirdly, this is my account, written under my name, and I'm not going to describe myself in someone else's terms; that is the very opposite of what I want to do.

What I will try to do instead is to convey my own understanding of autism and, as I tend to think in analogies, I will draw one for you now. I'll start by asking you to picture an AA road map of Great Britain (if you're under thirty-five, you might want to picture a Google map instead). This road map corresponds to the brain and nervous system of a non-autistic, or 'neurotypical', individual; there might be a few minor variations between individuals, but broadly speaking, most of the population is working with this sort of map. To make an autistic map, you first need to take out all the 'A' roads. Replace these with a selection of the other roads: motorways, 'B' roads, and the less well-travelled roads usually referred to as 'unclassified'. Any 'A' road could be replaced with any other kind of road, and the proportions will be different for every individual. You might get mostly 'B' roads and a handful of extra motorways, in which case you will probably strike people as remarkably talented but at the same time a little off, a little *odd*. On the other hand, you might lose out on the motorways altogether and end up with a baroque network of narrow, winding unclassifieds, slowing down and complicating your processing to the point where you experience significant difficulties with sensory input, emotional regulation, initiating action and motor planning; you may be unable to use spoken language at all, may also struggle with basic self-care, and will require a high level of support from others.

Most of us will fall somewhere between these two extremes, and no two of us will have the same map. What we have in common is that absence of 'A' roads – the standard ways of thinking, feeling, speaking and doing which non-autistic people share and can use to understand each other and navigate the world they've built for themselves. A 'B' road might be a close enough approximation, and will allow us to 'pass' in the world, but never completely, and never without considerable effort, or pain. If we think in terms of the social rather than the medical model of disability, we can see that while the 'unclassified' roads may represent real impairments, it is the lack of fit between the individual autistic map and the world of majority A-roaders that makes autistic people disabled. Autistic sociologist Damian Milton identifies this disabling lack of fit as the 'double empathy problem', which locates autistic people's social difficulties not in an inherent deficiency in social intelligence, but in the 'mutual incomprehension' which arises when people who think differently from each other try to communicate without adjusting for that difference.

It is this image of the variable map that I call to mind when I want to think about the wider autistic population, and why it might be that I feel so strongly that we *are* a distinct population, even though we vary so much among ourselves. Despite the variations between us, I find most autistic people easier to understand than most non-autistic people, just as Milton's theory would predict. At the same time, I would never claim to speak for us all. Quite apart from anything else, autistic people don't need me to. Ever since Temple Grandin and Donna Williams published the first 'autiebiographies' in the late eighties and early nineties, autistic people have been writing and sometimes also speaking for themselves. In the last few years, in the UK alone, we have seen the publication of autobiographies by Laura James, Katherine May, Chris Packham and Tom Cutler; Rhi Lloyd-Williams's play *The Duck*; Lana Grant's *From Here to Maternity: Pregnancy and Motherhood on the Autism Spectrum*; James McGrath's *Naming Adult Autism: Culture, Science, Identity*, a critique of the cultural myth which equates autism with a talent for STEM subjects and a lack of interest or ability in writing; poetry, including work by Kate Fox, Peter Street and the late Caron Freeborn, and my own *The Autistic Alice*. As I write, an excellent anthology, *Stim*, has just come out, edited by Lizzie Huxley-Jones, Elle McNicoll's children's book *A Kind of Spark* has been promoted by Waterstones and Dara McAnulty's *Diary of a Young Naturalist* has been winning both acclaim and prizes. (I'm sure I'll have left people out. Apologies to them.)

What I'm trying to get at is that I'm not writing this letter to prove to you that autistic people can write: it's very well established that we can. Being autistic is not the same as being 'nonverbal'. That term – 'nonverbal' – is so vague as to be misleading. Receptive language skills are not the same as expressive ones (I find it hard to employ both at the same time, which makes conversing with more than one or two other people very difficult for me. Lecturing, appearing at book festivals etc. – please note: not a problem.) Reading is not the same activity as listening. Speaking requires a very different set of skills from writing: there is a sub-group of autistic people who can use spoken language very little or not at all, but can use alternative and augmentative communication (AAC) methods to communicate. Some simply need access to a keyboard; others, who have difficulties with motor planning, require assistance to access AAC technology. Some of the most influential and innovative autistic advocates, such as Amy Sequenzia and the late, much-mourned Mel Baggs, have come out of this sub-group. Sequenzia, along with Elizabeth J. Grace, edited the anthology *Typed Words, Loud Voices*, which gathers together writing by non-speaking autistic people, alongside work by non-autistic people whose own disabilities make it difficult for them to speak. I would encourage you to read it.

And take care that your reading includes accounts by Black autistic people: Anand Prahlad's *The Secret Life of a Black Aspie* would be a good title to start with. You'll have a very partial picture if you don't. The classic image of the autistic person is someone like Joe from the BBC drama *The 'A' Word*: school age, male and white. For those of us who are either not male, not white, or neither male nor white, the persistence of this image stands in the way of diagnosis and support. For those of us who went to school in the fifties, sixties, seventies or eighties (or earlier) and did not fit the profile of 'classic autistic' with little or no speech and high support needs, no diagnosis existed. I was diagnosed at forty-two: that's not unusual. For the families of Black, Asian and Minority Ethnic children, early diagnosis remains hard to obtain, partly because of cultural biases in the way that largely white professionals interpret those children's behaviour. This same cultural bias means that the social consequences of autism, diagnosed or not, can be more serious for BAME children and adults. If I, a white middle-aged woman, behave oddly in public, people may avoid or laugh at me, but they are unlikely to call the police. If I were black and male as well as autistic, on the other hand, I would put myself in danger – real, physical danger – every time I left the house. It's important to acknowledge this. As the black lesbian feminist Audre Lorde put it, 'There is no such thing as a single-issue struggle, because we do not live single-issue lives.'[2]

I've taken that quote from Lorde's talk 'Learning from the 60s', in which she reflected back on her life as an activist. It had in many ways proved a frustrating and disappointing time. Lorde had come to realize that, when she moved in feminist circles, her particular concerns and experiences as a black American woman were pushed to the bottom of the agenda; in the male-dominated anti-racist movements, women's concerns were ignored. Both groups, in fact, were replicating at least some of the structural inequalities of the culture they claimed to want to change: white women decreed what feminism was, and black men decreed what was central to the struggle for civil rights.

This wasn't a problem only for black women, but, ultimately, for anybody who sought to see the world for what it is and to make it better. What Lorde and other black feminists such as bell hooks, Alice Walker and Toni Morrison realized was that the more dehumanized groups a person belongs to, the more their experience forces them to understand about the way society is structured: what and who it takes for granted, the truths about itself it chooses to ignore, who is doing the truly essential work. They showed how the different strands of inequality and injustice are knotted together into a net that holds us all, and that there's a limit to what you can accomplish if you focus only on the one string. Over the last few years, Lorde's writings have become for me what the writer Sara Ahmed terms 'feminist bricks': the theoretical and methodological supports on which I've come to base my work. Sara Ahmed's own writings, and especially her book *Living a Feminist Life*,[3] are also feminist bricks for me. Lorde and Ahmed, more than anyone else, have enabled me to see the specificities of my own condition, and to be more aware of its limitations when it comes to understanding the conditions of others. They have also shown me how to think from my own condition as a member of a specific marginalized group – disabled women in general, autistic women in particular – to examine my experience for what it can tell me about how the world really is, and how I might communicate what I have learned. Reader, if you haven't read Lorde and Ahmed yet, you really must. And everyone should read the paper in which Kimberle Crenshaw first set out the concept of 'intersectionality'. Originally coined by Crenshaw to enable analysis of the multidimensional nature of discrimination faced by black women, it has come to be the word most commonly used to remind everyone that, where structural inequality is concerned, there are no single-issue problems.[4]

Before I finish recommending other people's work, there are a couple more books I should mention, because, like the feminist brick writings, they were books that I needed to read before I could think of writing this one. The first will probably be very well known to you: it's *NeuroTribes* by Steve Silberman. *NeuroTribes* is a detailed and fascinating medical, social and cultural history of autism. In the first chapter, 'The Wizard of Clapham Common', Silberman gestures towards autism's possible pre-history, considering the life, work and character of the eighteenth-century 'natural philosopher' Henry Cavendish, and other famous figures such as Paul Dirac. Both Cavendish and Dirac were brilliant scientists who behaved very oddly, and each was 'a walking riddle to everyone who crossed his path'.[5] To be clear, Silberman is not diagnosing these men with autism – you cannot, and you should not, diagnose someone posthumously – but, if you are working on the assumption that the kind of people we now call autistic have always existed, then it is not unreasonable to wonder who these weird or uncanny individuals might have been, what sort of lives they led, and how the worlds they lived in responded to them.

I wanted to know who the weird women were – who were these weird sisters of mine? What sort of lives did they lead? How did the world respond to them? I was interested in the ways that autism – or weirdness, to give it a non-diagnostic term – might intersect with womanhood and with the norms of femininity. Since my diagnosis, I have been able to look back over my life from this new perspective, from this particular intersection, and it seemed to me that many of the moments when my autism had caused problems, or at least marked me out as different, were those moments when I had come up against some unspoken law about how a girl or a woman should be, and failed to meet it. I recently read an interview with the comedian Hannah Gadsby, and some of the experiences she shared were very familiar to me:

> Women with autism are a really interesting demographic. Until I had the diagnosis, I thought, Yeah, I'm a butch lesbian. But everything that makes me butch are decisions I made because of sensitivities or logic that have to do with my autism. I don't wear frills, because if I wear frills I think about it all day. I can't grow my hair, because if I have my hair around my face I think about it all day. There's a lot

about me that people are like, 'Ah, look, lesbian,' and really it's about me not wanting to think about my physical self so I can just get on with things.[6]

Women with autism are a varied demographic as well as an interesting one. Unlike Gadsby, I'm straight, and you wouldn't call me butch. But I've also made decisions about my appearance which are based on my autism: I hardly ever wear make-up, because it feels claggy and it smells; I can cope with frills but not lace next to my skin (women's underwear is a nightmare); I hate jewellery that shines too aggressively, or that moves in any way (charm bracelets make me gag); I don't wear heels, because I hate that clickety-clackety noise they make. Bangles are out because they roll up and down the arm. Wrap skirts and dresses are out because I can never figure out how to tie them. And I cannot – I WILL not – wear anything with metal buttons. So when I read the interview, I thought: 'Hello, Weird Sister.'

Autistic women are a minority demographic, and when you're in a minority, it can get lonely – your people are scarce and hard to find. The internet has helped many of us to find each other, and allowed us to group together, and to begin to discover that collective voice which any group needs if it's going to be heard. Some of these weird siblings, like Mel Baggs, have always spoken as autistic people; others, like Gadsby, had a public platform before diagnosis and have since used that platform to talk about their autism. Together, we can figure out what it means to be an autistic woman and communicate this to the world. There are two sides to this: on the one hand, we are explaining ourselves to the world; on the other hand, we are showing the world what it looks like to us. Here's Hannah Gadsby again:

there's still a lot of anxiety that comes with autism. I can be inadvertently rude, and that worries me. I don't want to be. That's why I study people. I know what people are going to do before they're going to do it... I think autism gets easier in a sense as you get older because you have more information. You're collecting the data.

At the time of writing, I have collected fifty years' worth of data about the non-autistic world: its attitudes, its assumptions, its expectations; its unwritten, unspoken rules. I have had to figure out this world and explain it to myself in explicit terms, so that I can navigate it (the 'A' roads I don't have) with the minimum number of accidents. It's been a matter of bare survival, but it's been enjoyable too: I like collecting data, finding patterns in it and drawing conclusions from the patterns. I draw reassurance from that, but also real joy.

There's also much reassurance, and much joy, to be had from locating a weird sister. So it was only natural that, in search of data and sisters, I should go the library and start scanning through books for traces of historical weird women. It's genealogy, but for my neurotype. I read about witches; I read about writers; I read about nuns, beguines and anchoresses; I read about women who had been shut up in institutions; I read about outcast girls and pathologized mothers. Sometimes I would read myself down a blind alley: anchoresses, for example, turned out not to be weird at all, but more akin to the medieval equivalent of the sort of modern woman who has raised her family and decided to retrain as a counsellor. I realized that the further back I went from my time, and the further away I went from my situation, the greater the chance of misinterpretation and misidentification. In the end, I identified four individuals who seemed to me to typify different aspects of life as a weird woman: Virginia Woolf, Adelheid Bloch, Frau V and Katharina Kepler. It was a very short list, and ultimately a very white and European list, but I hope that someone with a different perspective will be able to build on the work in this book, as I've been able to build on Silberman's work in *NeuroTribes*, and begin to fill in the many lives I've missed. There's a huge amount of work to do; this book is just one small part of it.

I have to say that I never meant to start this work by writing about Virginia Woolf. I had heard her spoken of as a candidate for weird womanhood, but I ruled her out. She is an exceptional figure, and I didn't want to write about exceptional figures. There are all kinds of people with a great deal invested in Woolf, and I didn't care to disturb them. I was aware of another writer, another deceased twentieth-century female writer, whose family had been greatly upset by suggestions that she might have been autistic. I could argue that there was no need for them to be upset, as there is nothing shameful about being autistic, but she was their relative, and they *were* upset. I would imagine that they were upset on two counts: firstly, because most people see autism as something that is wrong with a person, rather than different about them; secondly, because autism is seen as such a comprehensive explanation of a person that it threatens to reduce all their talent, effort and achievement to the status of a symptom, a kind of fortunate tic. I see things differently, but I know I'm in a minority, so I meant to stay away. But then I read Woolf's autobiographical writings, about the social discomfort of girlhood, and her lifelong complicated relationship with clothes and grooming, and they resonated so powerfully with me that I felt compelled to give over.

There was another reason why I had intended to avoid exceptional figures. There are plenty of books of feminist heroes, and they have their place, but this was never meant to be one of them. I was less interested in women who chose to be difficult than I was in women who couldn't help being weird. Weirdness is not the same as conscious rebellion or resistance, though it may come to inform it. I'm not doing that kind of feminism here. I'm also not doing the kind of autism advocacy based on the notion that we bring something special to the world. I don't want to have to argue that I'm special in order to justify my existence. That's not autism acceptance. Acceptance isn't about being celebrated: it's about being unremarked and unremarkable, the opposite of uncanny.

Exceptional status, like an autism diagnosis, is something that can obscure the ordinary in a person. Woolf had, for her time, very ordinary prejudices: she was a snob, she was racist, she was Anti-Semitic (I have no illusions about what she would have made of me) and she was an advocate of eugenics. She made it clear, in a horrific comment in her diary, that she thought people like my second weird woman, Adelheid Bloch, should be killed. Bloch was a German Jewish woman who had learning disabilities following a bout of childhood meningitis, and who had observable characteristics similar to those in people with autism diagnoses. Her life began in a comfortable household near Lake Constance, and ended in one of the prototype Nazi gas chambers, not because she was Jewish, but because she was disabled, the possessor of what her murderers termed 'a life unworthy of life'.

When I discovered that Bloch's difficulties arose as the result of brain damage, I had a moment of hesitation about whether she really belonged in this book, but then I realized that it was my hesitation, and not her precise status, that was causing problems. Remember how, at the beginning of this letter, I talked about human beings' strange preoccupation with drawing lines between themselves and other groups? We'll talk about 'what makes us human' and say it must be 'language' or 'empathy' or 'culture' or 'the capacity for thought' or 'the need for stories' – I could go on. The problem is that every single definition leaves some human beings out, and, as I've said again and again, when you are dehumanized, left outside the fold of the first person plural, then you are in danger – of social death, and also of the absolute, physical kind. So I kept Bloch with me. And with her, all the women who were non-speaking, who had high support needs, whose lives could not follow the usual prescribed pattern of women's lives, the sort of women who may now be diagnosed with autism or learning disabilities or both, but the categories don't matter as much as the women do. Too often a very hard line is drawn between autistic people like me, who are good at exams and IQ tests, and other autistic people who are not. It's an arbitrary and damaging line. In the second part of this book, I do my best to show how that line came into being, and take an eraser to it.

I've talked a great deal about feminist theory and feminist activism, but disability history, theory and activism are every bit as central to the work in this book. Without them, I could not have understood Bloch's story, or the story of the next woman, Frau V; I certainly could not have understood how their stories related to my own. When I write about erasing that arbitrary line, I am engaged in a 'dishuman' project. The concept of the dishuman was formulated by sociologists at the University of Sheffield,[7] and, according to the manifesto I have stuck to my wall, it is a concept that 'unpacks and troubles dominant notions of what it means to be human', with a view to replacing them with ideas that do not exclude or marginalize disabled people. If you flip to the back of this book, you'll find the full DisHuman Manifesto as an appendix. Katherine Runswick-Cole, one of the authors of the paper cited here, is the mother of an autistic person. So was

Frau V: I came across her in the paper Hans Asperger wrote in Austria in the forties, and which many decades later would be translated into English and inform the creation of a new diagnosis, Asperger's Syndrome. This diagnosis has been dropped from most manuals and has become very controversial, partly because it draws such a firm line between groups of autistic people, but also because Asperger was working in a child psychiatry clinic in Nazi-occupied Austria. Many of the children who passed through his clinic did not survive the war; how far Asperger colluded in this is a matter of much debate.[8] It has been suggested that he stressed the gifts of the children (all boys) in his paper on 'autistic psychopathy' as a way of saving them from the verdict of 'lives unworthy of life' and the fate that would follow. One of the case studies in this paper concerns one 'Franz V'. It offers a tantalizing glimpse of his mother, known only as 'Frau V', whose demeanour, appearance and habits suggest a very decided weirdness. Through Frau V, I was able to think about autistic mothering – mothering *by* autistic people – as well as autism mothering – the mothering *of* autistic people. Asperger, like many who came after him, saw autism as a largely male condition, but this did not stop him – or those who came after him – from pathologizing the mothers of autistic children. Then and now, mothers get blamed for everything. Both autistic mothers and autism mothers are particularly vulnerable to mother-blaming. And it is worth remembering that quite a few mothers belong to both groups.

The last of the four women, Katharina Kepler, who lived in early modern Germany, is also remembered because she was someone's mother. Her eldest son was the mathematician and astronomer Johannes Kepler, and it fell to him to defend her in a witch trial.[9] There is no evidence that Katharina practised witchcraft, but she lived in a time and a place where an accusation of witchcraft was a means of settling a score, and Katharina had an unfortunate habit of rubbing people up the wrong way. She did this by being assertive, forthright and persistent, by preferring rational argument to tears, and by refusing to bestow sympathy on someone just because they asked for it. I claim sisterhood with her on account of her resting bitch face (as described by Kepler), her habit of telling the truth as she saw it, and her failure to meet expectations with regard to eye contact. She reminds me a little of me, and a little of my mother. Even if you do not have a mother like Katharina, you have probably come across someone else who does. In a recent article in the *Guardian*, Patience Agbabi describes just such a mother:

> But who was she? After leaving my father, my brother and me, my mother lived in Nigeria from when I was 10 to 35, rarely visiting the UK. As early as I can remember, my mother struggled to maintain relationships with family, friends and colleagues because, in her words, 'They say I'm eccentric. And bossy.' She was inflexible, seeing everything in black and white. Either she fell out with people, or they fell out with her.[10]

The thing about 'bossy' women is they get the work done. There are things in the world that need fixing, and you cannot fix them without pointing out that they are broken; the fact that both the pointing out and the fixing makes comfortable people less comfortable is no reason not to do what you know to be right.[11]

So, these are my four weird sisters. I've introduced you to them, and, before I finish this letter, I also need to recommend one last book. It's by Georgina Kleege, and it's called *Blind Rage: Letters to Helen Keller*.[12] Growing up as a young blind girl, Kleege came to hate and resent Helen Keller, the deaf-blind woman held up to generations of D/deaf, blind and disabled children as a shining example of how to be and behave. Kleege wanted to take a closer look at the legend, to find the real, more complex person beneath. She could have written a straight biography, or a biography interspersed with memoir, but instead she wrote *to* Keller. This made sense: it was her relationship to Keller which needed rewriting, and therefore it was Keller she needed to write to.

Thanks to Kleege, I also realized that it was the weird women I needed to write *to*, and not just *about*. Weird women have been spoken about quite enough. We're all sick of it. I've said it before and I'll say it again: when people talk about you and not to you, it's dehumanizing. When people talk about you and not to you, they often leave themselves out of the picture, their humanity unquestioned and unexamined. They hide in the conveniently disembodied, sometimes passive, voice of the clinical report, the case review, the research paper. Weird women know far more than we want to about how we look to the world. We're tired of responding to its demands that we explain our difference ('Oh, you're autistic? How does it manifest itself?'). These letters are not about explaining ourselves to other people, but about explaining how it feels to live in a world other people built for themselves, and how that world and those people appear to us. This is the view not *into* Uncanny Valley, but *from* it.

Reader, this is the only letter in this book that is addressed to you, but you have my permission to read the others.

Weirdest regards,
Joanne

Virginia Woolf

Adeline Virginia Woolf (née Stephen; 25 January 1882–28 March 1941) was an English writer, a pioneering modernist whose work continues to influence both novelists and essayists. As a member of the Bloomsbury Group, Woolf lived in a world of cultural critics, journalists, diarists and prolific letter-writers where intense reflection – on oneself, on others, on one's relationship with those others – was expected and encouraged. As a result, her life is exceptionally well documented, both from within and without. It was a complex and often difficult life, and, alongside her complex and often difficult work, it lends itself to endless scholarship, interpretation and re-interpretation. As well as the pioneering modernist Woolf, you can find the feminist Woolf, the bipolar Woolf, the traumatized Woolf, the lesbian Woolf, the asexual Woolf, the gender-fluid Woolf. None of these is a misinterpretation; none of these is wholly definitive. Such is the richness of both the life and work combined that you could say, as a Jewish sage once said of the Torah and its interpretation, 'Turn it, and turn it, for everything is in it.' In this letter I turn it again, and find a Woolf with whom I can identify.

Letter to Virginia Woolf

Dear Mrs Woolf

Beginning an unsolicited letter to a stranger is a very unnerving thing to do. It's like knocking on the door of a room you've never entered before, without an invitation. I think that you'd recognize the uneasy sensations that I'm experiencing now as the kind a woman might feel as she steps into a room full of unfamiliar people, knowing that the moment she crosses that threshold everything about her – her clothes, her hair, her face, her expression, her way of holding herself, the extent to which she talks and the manner in which she does so – will be subjected to the most intense and minute scrutiny. Every new room is an examination room, and there are so many ways to fail.

I know that you lived that moment many times, and I know because you kept coming back to it in your writing; describing it was one small part of your great life's project, to try and find a language for all the kinds of moments that make up human existence – and women's existence especially. You understood that it is the accumulation of moments, however trivial they were in themselves, that can determine the course of a life. Your novels explore all the different ways in which a writer might delineate these moments and arrange them to show their relationship to each other, so that the reader might discern in that arrangement the shape of a character's lived experience.

Your novels were written for public consumption. When you wrote more directly of the experiences that fed them, I imagine you meant your writing to be private. I can easily believe that if you knew that your diaries, and your letters, and the autobiographical pieces you wrote for your Bloomsbury friends had been collected and edited and sent out for public scrutiny, a part of you would be mortified. Yes, you were a forward-thinking bohemian who took risks in her life and her writing; you were a biographer yourself, and the daughter of a biographer. But you were also the daughter of a woman who brought you up to be a discreet, dignified, upper-middle-class Victorian lady, and I don't think you ever managed completely to shake off this training. (It is out of respect for this Victorian lady that I could not bring myself to address you as 'Virginia'). Your mother died young, and she haunted you. She haunted your grand project, the call you had to describe women's experience, and your reading of her life informed the feminism that drove that project. I've read *A Room of One's Own*, and I'm thinking of that sentence from it that's quoted so often: 'For we think back through our mothers if we are women.'[13] By which you meant not only our mothers literal, but also our mothers metaphorical. All the mothers, including our literary ones.

So, without your permission, but in the spirit of feminism, I'm going to think back through you, through the living trace of you as it appears in your own words and the words of others. I won't be the first writer to do so. I certainly won't be the last. Since you stopped living in your body and made a more permanent home in your texts, you have been working at a rate that no breathing version of you could ever match. You do so much representing for people; you do so much standing for things. You are a writer's writer, a modernist, a modernist writer, a feminist, a woman modernist writer, a modernist feminist writer, a bipolar patient, a depressive, a sexual abuse survivor, a PTSD sufferer, a lesbian, a bisexual woman; *Orlando* and your relationship with the woman who inspired it have made you a significant figure in the discourse around queerness and gender; your privilege has made you emblematic of the limitations of white middle-class feminism; the way you talked about the women who worked for you, the snobbery you showed in your treatment of certain characters (we'll come back to that) and certain writers has led to your being derided as the embodiment of the elitist tendencies of literary fiction. You're the woman writer's woman's writer, but also the elitist's elitist (who didn't get Joyce). And now I've got some more work for you to do.

I want to start by visiting some of those unnerving moments I've been talking about: those moments when you stood on a threshold, waiting to be judged. As you tell it, you suffered many of the most bruising ones when you were still Virginia Stephen, living at the family home at Hyde Park Gate, in the years between the deaths of your parents, when 'the pressure of Victorian society' on you and your sister Vanessa was at its strongest. This pressure took solid human form in the person of your older half-brother George Duckworth, who took it upon himself to launch you into society, dragging you through a succession of Victorian social examination rooms, in which he was always Chief Examiner. You were both beautiful girls – beautiful, well-connected girls – and George had every reason, on the face of it, to believe that your presence at his side would enhance his social capital.

He was wrong. Not about your being beautiful, or well con-nected, but in his assumption that you must want the kind of success that he wanted, or have enough interest in his success to sacrifice yourselves upon its altar. He tried with Vanessa first, but she resisted him, and fought him, and although George turned 'every battery' of emotional blackmail upon her, she resisted, and she fought, and ultimately she prevailed. So one morning he came to see you in your room, interrupted you in the middle of your Greek, gave you an ugly jewel as a present, and after a strategic silence, proceeded to tell you how much suffering Vanessa was causing. And not just to him – but also to the younger Duckworth brother, Gerald. For how could either Duckworth bring ladies back to the house, without a lady present to receive them? What were they to do? Your dearest mother had been the lady, but she was dead; then Stella Duckworth, his sister, had taken her place, but she had married, and left, and quickly died in her turn. So that left only the Stephen girls, you and Vanessa, and Vanessa was being perfectly monstrous. So it followed that, if you could not help, both George and Gerald, starved of more fitting and well-behaved female company, must be driven into the arms of prostitutes. The fate of the whole household was in your hands – so was it to be ruin and degradation for everyone, or would you accompany him to a Dowager Marchioness's ball?

You agreed – for how could you not? – and your examination season began. As I have said, your Chief Examiner was George Duckworth himself. Every evening, you would have to pass through a succession of rooms in which your appearance, demeanour, speech and conduct were to be scrutinized and judged against the most exacting standards; every evening, the first room you passed through would be your own drawing-room at Hyde Park Gate, the first judge was always George, and his standards the most exacting of all. It was unfair of him to have been so inflexible: he must have been aware of your financial situation, and known that you lacked the means to equip yourself for the kind of society he hoped to impress. Even when you were not going out, you and Vanessa were expected to present yourselves in that drawing-room at eight o'clock, with your arms and necks bare, ready to receive. The collision of society's (or George's) inexorable demands and your limited financial circumstances must have led to so many jarring moments; you describe one in 'A Sketch of the Past'; and even after forty years it still made you sick with shame:

I would stand in front of George's Chippendale glass trying to make myself not only tidy but presentable. On an allowance of fifty pounds it was difficult, even for the skilful, to be well dressed of an evening. For though a house dress could be made by Jane Bride, at a cost of a pound or two, a party dress cost perhaps fifteen guineas if made by Mrs Young. The house dress therefore might be, as on this particular night, made of a green stuff bought erratically at a furniture shop – Story's – because it was cheaper than dress stuff; also more adventurous. Down I came: in my green evening dress; all the lights were up in the drawing room; and there was George, in his black tie and evening jacket, in the chair by the fire. He fixed on me that extraordinary observant [illegible] gaze with which he always inspected clothes. He looked me up and down as if [I] were a horse turned into the ring. Then the sullen look came over him; a look in which one traced not merely aesthetic disapproval; but something that went deeper; morally, socially, he scented some kind of insurrection; of defiance of social standards. I was condemned from many more points of view than I can analyse as I stood there, conscious of those criticisms; and conscious too of fear, of shame and of despair – 'Go and tear it up', he said at last, in that curiously rasping and peevish voice which expressed his serious displeasure at this infringement of a code that meant more to him than he would admit.[14]

Yes, the shame comes through, but also defiance, an independence of mind, and a gaze to counter George's: as he inspected your dress and found it wanting, so you inspected his values and his character, and found them both to be ridiculous. And it is your judgement, not his, that has survived. You did not tear up the dress.

There are so many struggles going in this story: between shame and defiance; between Virginia Stephen and George Duckworth; between the nineteenth and twentieth centuries; between society's insistence on defining a girl and a girl's desire to define herself; between creativity and convention; between the Victorian lady your mother bred you to be and the inky-fingered writer who had the run of her father's library. I recognized them all as I read that passage, and although I am far from being a young Victorian lady of the upper-middle class, I identified with some of them too. I know what it is to put on clothes, to go out, to be looked up and down, and immediately 'condemned from more points of view than I can analyse'. When I was a girl, I thought I was being interesting with my clothes – but apparently all I was being was wrong.

You have your dress stories to tell; so do I. One is the story of a dress I bought and wore when I was in the sixth form. It was a short-sleeved shirtwaist, with a narrow self-tie belt, made of some artificial material, white with royal blue polka dots (there were a lot of polka dots in the eighties). I remember it so well, and the fluorescent pink towelling socks I was wearing with it (there was a lot of fluorescent pink then too), because they were what I had on that afternoon when I was walking home from school and found myself a few steps behind a pair of other girls in my year. I knew them, but not well: I was Clever; they were Cool. They were ambling along quite slowly, talking, and I was thinking of speeding up to go past them when I overheard a scrap of conversation. One of them was complaining about her lack of success with boys; she couldn't understand it, she said; it wasn't as if 'I dressed like *Joanne Limburg…!*'

At that point I must have stopped walking, and looked down at myself, which must be why I remember that dress – and those socks – so very well. As I remember it now, I can see what they saw: that I was wearing a cheap nylon old-lady dress, that the way it cut my legs off in the middle of their short calves was deeply unflattering, that the ankle socks truncated my legs still further, and that the section of leg that remained on view really should have been shaved. It would be tempting, for the sake of the narrative, to say that at that moment I experienced a defining epiphany that changed my wardrobe and my grooming forever, but that wouldn't be true. I think it's more likely that in that moment, I experienced mixed emotions similar to those you experienced when George told you to destroy your green dress: shame, yes, but also a more defiant feeling, that clothes should not be simply right or wrong; that there was no absolute reason why a dress should not be made of upholstery material, or a seventeen-year-old girl should not pair a nylon shirtwaist with a pair of fluorescent flannel socks, and it was irrational to behave as if there were. And then there was that other implication, that the function of a dress on a teenage girl could only be to enhance her attractiveness to men, and I think we both baulked at that.

Twelve years or so before I overheard the girls talking about me, and about eighty years after George sent you back upstairs to change, the feminist film-maker and writer Laura Mulvey wrote a paper exploring the concept of the 'male gaze'. Mulvey surveyed the history of cinema and saw a multitude of men looking through cameras at a multitude of women. By definition, as Mulvey and John Berger and others suggested, men look, and women are what they are looking at. George turned his 'male gaze' upon you, and exercised this unexamined, unquestioned power to define you solely in terms of what he saw, and how much it did or did not please him; to the extent that you internalized this male gaze, you felt shame. When you looked at yourself in the mirror in Hyde Park Gate at the turn of the last century, you were supposed to have been looking for an image of what George would see. When I looked at myself in the changing-room mirror in that dress shop in Edgware, I should have been looking not through my own eyes, but through the gaze of a teenage boy in eighties North West London. Unlike the two cool girls, I had failed to internalize that gaze. You could say that in failing to do that, I had failed to become a girl at all. As you had, that evening you descended the stairs not so much dressed as upholstered. A girl is made according to the requirements of that gaze, and we had neither of us put ourselves together in such a way as to meet those requirements.

And if you have failed to be a girl, then – heaven help you – you might as well be *anything*. When George looked at you, you were a horse in the ring. When a couple of boys walked past me that summer when I was seventeen and I made the compound mistake of a) wearing shapeless clothes and b) looking them in the eye, I was, apparently, a 'dog'.

You can find failed girl-critters in literature too. Stephen King's Carrie is one of the more grotesque examples. By page 7 of the novel named after her, she has already been described as a frog, a sacrificial goat, an ox, and a hog ripe for slaughter. These transformations occur in the course of one scene, during which she has her first period in the school showers. She is terrified, doesn't understand what is happening. The other girls mock her, pelting her with tampons and sanitary towels, and chanting '*Plug it up!*'[15] Her persecution is, King writes, inevitable, the result of pressure that has been building all the way through school, 'in accordance with all the laws that govern human nature, building with all the steadiness of a chain reaction approaching critical mass'.[16] When Carrie tries to escape this scapegoat role, accepts help from a girl who feels sorry for her, dresses up nicely and tries to 'get along with the world', to be a 'whole person', all that results is an even more violent and public humiliation: at the climax of the novel, she is doused in pig blood at her school prom. In her revenge she reveals herself to be, not a recognizable human after all, but a genetic mutant with telekinetic powers, which she uses for indiscriminate murder and destruction. In the end her mother dispatches her with a knife, as if she were indeed a hog to be slaughtered.

This all comes about because a popular, attractive girl, Sue Snell, has outraged the natural order by persuading her boyfriend to take Carrie to the prom, and bring the outcast in. Sue fails spectacularly, bringing harm to Carrie, herself and everyone around her. Instead of bringing Carrie into the fold, she finds herself cast out, a figure of blame. As I read the book, I assumed that Sue was the character who was supposed to embody the reader's – and author's – point of view, but I was also aware that many readers identify with Carrie and see her as a figure ripe with subversive potential. For these readers, she stands for disavowed female power. I identify with her too, but for me the identification is not empowering, but painful. To my mind, Carrie is created to be an abomination and she's in the novel to die. She's abjection personified. And, as Sue Snell learns, abjection is the condition that leads to social death. In *Carrie*, it is shown to be contagious.

If Carrie's social condition – or mine, at her age, or yours – were indeed contagious, it would provide an explanation for the discomfort that the presence of a Carrie-figure produces. Take the supernatural horror element away, and you are left with a harmless girl, overwhelmingly more sinned against than sinning. You'd think it would be the easiest thing in the world to leave her alone, but the girls in her gym class can't. The sight of Carrie sobbing and bleeding under the shower provokes disgust, which transforms into ridicule as they surround her, pelt her with sanitary towels and tampons, and scream at her, '*Plug it up!*' We see the scene from the perspective of Sue Snell, who 'gasped laughter from her nose and felt an odd, vexing mixture of hate, revulsion, exasperation and pity'.[17] The sight of Carrie gormlessly unplugged leads to an unplugging of Sue's own disavowed, unladylike feelings, and laughter escapes gracelessly, piggishly, from her nicely powdered nose. Sue's feelings vex her because they are nasty, unpredictable and uncontrolled, the kind of feelings that are unpleasantly surprising to a girl who wishes to think of herself – and who doesn't? – as a nice person. Her kind actions towards Carrie are motivated, not by genuine empathy, but by a desire to earn back her own good opinion of herself: to be a young lady again, and not a pig.

In describing Sue Snell's discomfort, Stephen King was expressing his own. He tells the story in his memoir *On Writing*, and again in the introduction to an edition of the novel. The seeds of *Carrie* lay in his memories of two girls he knew growing up, a pair of wrongly dressed misfits who were picked on all the way through school. King describes how one of these girls, named as 'Tina' in one text and 'Dodie' in the other, tried to escape

her designated place at the bottom of the pecking order. Tina/
Dodie came from an eccentric family, which could have been bad
enough in itself, but what made her a focus of ridicule was that
she wore the same outfit to school every single day. King writes:

> I can still see that outfit; I don't even need to close my
> eyes. There was the red hairband over the black (and
> really quite beautiful) hair. There was the white sleeveless
> blouse, worn both summer and winter, clinging ever more
> tightly to the growing and quite heavy bosom. And there
> was the black skirt, falling gracelessly to the lower part of
> the shin.[18]

And there we have Tina/Dodie, an object that disturbs by
being desirable and repellent all at once, fixed forever in the gaze
of a teenage boy.

One autumn, Tina/Dodie – like Carrie – made a bid to
change her story. She came into school wearing a new outfit. King
doesn't remember the details of the new ensemble, 'only how
happy she was to be wearing it'. But her hopes for a new version
of her life were short-lived. He goes on: 'I can *clearly* remember
how her hopeful vivacity changed – first into surprise, then into
anger, and finally into dull acceptance – as the teasing and the
insults and the sarcastic comments rained down on her. Instead of
abating, the kids' rejection of Tina became even fiercer.' It wasn't,
after all, just the clothes, but something broader and less tangible,
'that broadcast STRANGE! NOT LIKE US! KEEP AWAY!' The
older King suggests that this message is broadcast on 'a wave-
length only other kids can pick up', and that as an adult he can
remember it, but not feel it. I don't agree with him about that:
I think adults do continue to receive the transmission but, if

maturity has done its work, they learn to inhibit their responses to it. And if they reflect back on their teenage selves, as King is doing, they may wish they had behaved differently. King, who, like Sue Snell, did not participate in the bullying but did not stand up to it either, is open about the guilt and discomfort he feels as he remembers these two girls. Neither would finish high school, and neither would live into her thirties: one would die from a seizure, the other by suicide. Like Carrie, they died young; unlike Carrie, they didn't get their revenge in first.

King confesses that, despite the success of *Carrie* and all that came after it, he has never felt comfortable with the novel, its central character, or the memories which inspired them. In *On Writing*, he says that 'I never liked Carrie, that female version of Eric Harris and Dylan Klebold, but through Sondra and Dodie I came at last to understand her a little. I pitied her and I pitied her classmates as well, because I had been one of them once upon a time.'[19] As I read this, and noted the comparison to the Columbine killers, it occurred to me that I had never heard of a real female version of Harris and Klebold. I have never come across a female self-described 'incel' who goes on the rampage and kills the attractive men who've spurned her. I can remember feeling that I was repellent to attractive men; I never felt that they were denying me my rights, only that they'd seen something disgusting in me and that the proper response on my part was to hide and feel ashamed. Perhaps by describing Carrie as a Klebold figure, and by giving her the telekinetic gift which is the overt source of horror in the novel, King is trying enact revenge on behalf of the girls who haunt him, while at the same time giving form to his teenage sense that there was indeed something about them that was dangerous and abhorrent. In which case, the persecution they faced was not persecution at all, but only self-defence.

I can't imagine that you would be a great King reader (though I'm always prepared to be wrong). But I could see you reading Margaret Drabble. If you read her debut novel, *A Summer Bird-Cage*, published in 1963, you'd find Daphne, another memorable failed girl-critter. Daphne has no psychic powers, and is ignored rather than persecuted, but, in common with Carrie, she has one very intriguing quality: the power to make her creator uncomfortable.

Like so many female novelists writing in English, Drabble is in your debt, and she has acknowledged it. In her 1972 essay 'How Not to Be Afraid of Virginia Woolf', she tells the reader that for a long time she was put off by your elitist reputation, but then she came across *A Room of One's Own*. She read it 'with mounting excitement and enthusiasm. Could it be true that she herself had assembled these ideas that were my daily life?' There she was, sitting 'in my own room in Bloomsbury, feeling myself uncannily a product of [Virginia Woolf's] imagination'.[20] She recognized you as her mother, a figure she might think through.

And today I recognize how much I've benefitted from all the mothers that came after you: I've had Drabble to think through. That term 'feeling myself uncannily a product of [a writer's] imagination' is, like so many of her descriptions of inner states, quite wonderfully precise. It captures so perfectly that excitement of reading a text and encountering yourself in it; the excitement that comes from feeling that, through the medium of that text, you have made a real and living connection to the person who wrote it. More than a connection, even – at that point, you merge, recapture the state which Marion Milner described as 'undifferentiation' and Freud, more warily, as 'the oceanic feeling'. That sentence you just read – it is not only part of a text, but also part of you, and part of the person who wrote it, *all at the same time*.

After I published *The Woman Who Thought Too Much*, I began to receive messages from people telling me that I had been writing not only about my life but theirs, not only about myself but also about them – that *they felt as if we were the same person*. If they were deluded, it was in the most benign possible way. When you have this kind of reading experience with a text, you fuse with it, and it becomes part of you forever. It is, more often than not, a positive alteration.

Sometimes, though, a fragment of text can become lodged in a reader in a less benign way. These textual fragments remain other, remain as foreign bodies; they itch, they prod, they nag, they trouble; they will not rest in place; they persecute their hosts. I have also had this kind of experience with Drabble's writing, when I first read *A Summer Bird-Cage* in my late teens, and Daphne lodged in me like a splinter.

I must have been in my late teens. I had read quite a bit of Drabble by then. *Jerusalem the Golden* came first. I loved that book, and still do. I loved its protagonist, Clara, although I knew I had no hope of ever being her – she was too bold, too socially capable, too confident in her attractiveness for me ever to take her as a model. Over the next few years, I read more Drabble. First *The Millstone*, then *The Garrick Year* and after that *The Waterfall*. Then I circled back to *A Summer Bird-Cage*.

The novel's protagonist and narrator, Sarah, is a young woman living in the early sixties. She has just left Oxford with a 'shiny new useless' first class degree, which she does not know what to do with. What she does know is that she is fortunate: she is privileged, clever, well educated and lovely-looking. She is not, however, as lovely as her poised, beautiful older sister Louise, next to whom she always feels grubby, ordinary and little-sisterish. When her feelings of inferiority become too difficult to bear, Sarah can console herself with the fact that Louise only managed an upper second at Oxford. Sarah ascribes her sister's relative underachievement to her having chosen the wrong subject, and, as the novel begins, Louise is about to act on another apparently perverse decision: she is going to marry a rich but dislikeable man, whom she does not seem to love. Sarah has come home from France to be her sister's bridesmaid. The other bridesmaid is their cousin Daphne.

We know what Daphne's role is to be before we even meet her. She comes up in the first conversation between the lovely, clever sisters. In answer to Sarah's question about how the wedding preparations are going, Louise complains of Daphne's presence in the family home. She speaks 'in tones of such disdain that she might have been talking about an earwig, not a first cousin'.[21] Another failed girl-critter to join Carrie and me at the zoo. And an earwig of all things: something brown and disgusting that scuttles out from under a skirting-board, verminous and always out of place.

Louise and Sarah are quite emphatically *not* failed girls, and throughout the book they define themselves in terms of their difference from Daphne. Even when she is not an earwig, she is something quite different in kind from her cousins. Later on in that first conversation, Sarah worries that her dress, which has been made in her absence, might not fit. Louise responds: 'Oh well, never mind… you can't look worse than Daphne anyway, can you?'[22] Daphne is the girl both sisters are relieved not to be. At other times, she is the girl Sarah fears herself to be. As the wedding approaches, she reflects on her time at Oxford, when she at last emerged from Louise's shadow:

> I was always a one for seeing things in extremes, and because I wasn't as beautiful as Louise I assumed I was as plain as Daphne: whereas in fact if there is a barrier

down the middle of mankind dividing the sheep from the goats I am certainly on Louise's side of it as far as physical beauty goes.[23]

Sheep and goats. The saved and the damned. The goats are the girls you are relieved not to be. *If I dressed like Joanne Limburg…*

But what if it isn't how one dresses? What if, as in the Tina/Dodie story, it is something essential that damns a girl, something it will never be in her power to change? Throughout the novel, every time Daphne appears, Sarah puzzles over exactly what it is that makes Daphne so unfortunate – is it frumpiness or plainness, and can the two ever really be untangled? How can she, Sarah, ever really be certain that she is in no danger of becoming Daphne? At one point, Sarah is going round the Tate Gallery with a male companion, when she catches sight of Daphne, smartly but unflatteringly dressed, and 'looking so like herself and what she was that she seemed a cross between a symbol and a cartoon'.[24]

After Daphne has tried, unsuccessfully, to flirt with Sarah's friend, and they have seen her into a taxi, they discuss her appearance. He says, of her clothes:

'I must say it was a curious colour-scheme.'

'Very curious.' I looked at his delicately narrowed trousers, his expensive suede jacket, and his pretty green tie. 'Don't you think she could do better if she tried?' I said.

'Why should she try? It wouldn't help,' he said…[25]

As the pair walk along the Embankment, Sarah watches a glamorous, laughing couple go by in a speedboat, and immediately feels 'stagnant and covered in oil and dead feathers, to see them there'. She understands this as the after-effect of meeting her cousin, because 'Daphne is somehow a threat to my existence. Whenever I see her, I feel weighted down to earth. I feel the future narrowing before me like a tunnel, and everyone else is high up and laughing.'[26]

Like Carrie, Daphne seems to harbour within her body some kind of terrible social contagion, and Sarah's familial closeness to this 'cross between a symbol and a cartoon'[27] endangers her own standing in the world, opens her up to the possibility of ostracism and ridicule by association. She reminds Sarah of what social failure looks like, and reminds her that there is no guarantee that she herself will not fail, become an abject creature, sticky and decaying. If Sarah does not keep putting herself together to meet the requirements of girlhood, if she slips up in any way, she may yet become Daphne.

Just as Carrie and Daphne cause discomfort by acting as symbols of abjection and failure, they both cause further unease by bringing out the ugly thoughts and feelings that threaten other girls' images of themselves as nice and good. A pretty girl should, ideally, be pretty on the inside too. People will find out if she is not. Pleasant feelings make a girl look sweet and approachable; unpleasant ones screw up the mouth, narrow the eyes and crease the brow. The lack of a pleasant expression on a girl's face is as much a faux pas as Daphne's frumpy gallery outfit. When I was younger, I was always being told to smile by strangers in the street – specifically, male strangers: *Smile, love – it might never happen!* One man said this to me a week after my miscarriage; I didn't have the energy to point out to him that it already had.

Sarah knows, as all girls do, that her purpose is to be nice. On the day of Louise's wedding, she considers Daphne in her bridesmaid's get-up, and appals herself:

When we arrived at the church there was a crowd of villagers standing round the nineteen-thirty lych-gate staring, and I wondered if she realized that they were probably saying things like: 'A pity she isn't as good-looking as the rest of the family' or 'You always get one plain bridesmaid, don't you?' I don't know if Daphne cares about her looks at all: I fear she probably does, because her clothes, though hideous, are always elaborate, not careless, and she over-curls her hair and wears a very bright red lipstick which makes her skin look pale and dead. She wears it in an effort to appear gay. How unjust life is, to make physical charm so immediately apparent or absent, when one can get away with vices untold forever... Daphne inflicts such pain on me. She makes me confess how much I am a bitch.[28]

Daphne is doing nothing to Sarah, while Sarah thinks unkind thoughts about Daphne, but it is Daphne, not Sarah, who is described as 'inflicting pain'. Although Sarah is a sophisticated enough narrator to be saying this with a certain irony, she is also expressing something that she genuinely feels.

Daphne is doing something terribly wrong, something that not only blights her own girlhood, but also casts a shadow over girls around her too. Again, like Carrie, she is an incompetent manager of her body; she fails to 'plug it up'. Later, sitting next to Daphne in the church, Sarah can't help noticing how the brides-maid's dress which suits her makes her cousin look 'a total fright'. She reflects that 'I have nice legs, whereas Daphne's are muscular and shapeless round the ankles and covered in hairs and bluish pimples. Oh, the agony. If I had any courage I would have told her to put on suntan stockings, but somehow I couldn't interfere with the awfulness of nature.'[29]

*

I told you earlier how Daphne had lodged in me like a splinter. It was that image of her legs that did it. Mine are not shapeless, but they are short, and when I first encountered Daphne, I had convinced myself that this fact alone was enough to condemn me. I also have dark leg hair over pale skin, so I have three options: remove it with the utmost thoroughness and frequency, cover it up, or show it and risk disgust. I hit puberty early, but for a long time I couldn't bring myself to face the complex practicalities of hair-removal, and tights felt horrible, so I hung onto my knee socks. I hung onto them until I was fourteen. I remember the day I realized I had to ditch them. It was another of those moments. I was playing a circle game with some other girls in a drama group at school, a spoken version of Consequences, in which we had to keep adding to a description of an imaginary character, which got longer and longer as it moved around the circle. We created a character, we added hair, and height, and clothes, and then we got to legwear. At which point, someone suggested, 'White knee socks!' and everyone from my class sniggered except me. In that moment I understood that I had for a horribly long time failed to plug up the awfulness of nature, and everyone but me had been able to watch it seeping out of my person.

I dropped the knee socks, much to my mother's relief. I began to wear pop-socks instead. I was scared of razors, so I hesitated over what to do about the hair for a couple of years, until I discovered Immac. It was ineffective and it smelled like cat sick, but at least I knew I was trying. I've been shaving for years now, but I'm still haunted by Daphne's legs. Every time I see a stray leg hair, no matter how insignificant, there she is, reminding me that I'm her and she's Carrie and that the three of us deserve nothing but shame. The whole point of the work that goes into the presentation of girlhood and then womanhood is to erase itself, and by doing it incompetently we are drawing attention to it, and to the unruly animal body – 'the awfulness of nature' – it is meant to conceal. After all, Sarah has presumably had to shave her own legs. Even the models in the Gillette adverts, ever-smiling as they slide their razors quite unnecessarily down marble-smooth calves, have undergone some kind of depilatory process off-screen. It's only us failed girls who give the game away – that, to paraphrase Eimear McBride, a girl is a made-up thing.

Girlishness is made up not only on the outside, but on the inside too. When one girl gives the game away, the other girls will pull off their masks and show their teeth. The 'awfulness of nature' that Sarah perceives refers not only to Daphne's hairiness, but also to the brutal pecking order which has Daphne at the bottom, and Sarah and Louise as the greedier, healthier animals who are compelled to knock her down. Later in the novel, Louise invokes the idea of a natural order quite explicitly, describing Daphne as one of the social 'herbivores' whose lowly existence is necessary in order to maintain the superior existence of 'carnivores' such as herself and Sarah. Daphne's social ostracism, like Carrie's humiliation, is seen as the inevitable result of a process of natural selection.

Remember I said that Daphne made Drabble uncomfortable? When I re-read *A Summer Bird-Cage* not that long ago, I came across a set of 'annotations' on the first edition Drabble had written for the *Guardian* in 2013. In 'Re-reading in 2012: Observations', she wrote: 'The portrait of cousin Daphne is unforgivable – I'm ashamed of it.'[30] It's a striking admission, suggesting a certain lack of distance between Sarah and the younger Drabble, and it's worth bearing in mind that Drabble was still only twenty-four when the novel was published. She was already married with children – the state which Sarah understands to be the generally desired outcome of successful girlhood – but she may still have felt too afraid of her own ultimate fate to be generous to a character who represented her fears. Ellen Z. Lambert says as much in her essay on *A Summer Bird-Cage*, and notes that later Drabble heroines, more mature and less fearful, are able to respond more generously to 'incomplete creatures' like Daphne.[31] As older, more established, successful women, they know what Sarah cannot, which is that they will never now be transformed into the sort of woman which Daphne represents.

I'm twice the age Drabble was when she created Daphne, and I would agree that if one survives this long, then the fear of abject social failure is less acute, but if there is a point where a woman might feel established and successful *as* a woman, I haven't reached it yet. As you grew older, you noted in yourself that this fear did diminish, but never disappeared, something you acknowledged in a diary entry you wrote in your early thirties:

> We both went up to London this afternoon; L. to the Library, & I to ramble about the West End, picking up clothes. I am really in rags. It is very amusing. With age too one's less afraid of the superb shop women. These great shops are like fairies' palaces now. I swept about in Debenham's & Marshall's & so on, buying as I thought with great discretion. The shop women are often very charming, in spite of their serpentine coils of black hair.[32]

The first thing I do when I read this is flinch at the words 'shop women' – snobby Mrs Woolf! – but I don't think you mean to be insulting. Nor do I think that you are being sarcastic when you call them 'superb'. Their grooming, so obviously more expert, more correctly feminine than yours, makes you feel inferior, less secure in a space that is theirs and that they occupy so confidently: it is the shop and they are the shop women. At this point in your life, you are 'less afraid', but not unafraid, and you have learned to pre-empt any possibility of ridicule by ridiculing yourself first: 'I am really in rags. It is very amusing.'

For me, this vignette of your shopping trip is another one of those mothering moments from your autobiographical writings which I can take up, place next to the scene with George, and use to think through. For 'serpentine coils of black hair', I might substitute: shiny, straight hair, make-up perfectly applied, thickened eyelashes, sharply drawn eyebrows and full sets of long, unbroken, glossy nails. Next to today's fashion retail workers (*not* 'shop women'!), I look and feel, like you, that I am 'really in rags'. Made of rags, in fact – with the possible addition of crude oil, feathers and past-its-use-by sacrificial hogmeat. At least now I can put some of the difference down to age. When I was the same age as the girls who took my money in Topshop and Miss Selfridge, it was just inferiority – Daphne-ness, Carrie-ness, plain and simple.

As Sarah and Sue Snell both discover, the worst aspect of a Carrie or a Daphne is not anything they do (let's put the telekinetic massacre aside for one moment), but what their presence evokes in the psyches of the other women around them. If a girl or a woman has the slightest smidgen of disgust about her body or fears about her social status – and pretty well all girls and women do – a Carrie or a Daphne will reflect it back to her, horribly magnified. None of us could ever be as pretty and nice and odourless inside and out as good girls and nice women are supposed to be, as we are supposed to be by definition. Any girl or woman who suspects herself to be anything other than perfectly pretty, nice and odourless inside and out risks not being a girl or a woman at all. And, as I've been saying, if you are not a woman or a girl, then you might as well be anything – any manner of kickable monstrosity. No wonder still-viable girls want to distance themselves from the visibly failed ones.

Since I don't want to lie to you, or to myself, I should admit at this point that I have not been at every moment of my life in the Daphne-position. I have had my moments of being Sarah, and I have had shameful moments when I have worked to manoeuvre myself as close to Sarah and as far away from Daphne as I can. Drabble's ashamed of Daphne. I'm ashamed of a poem I wrote in my twenties. Called 'The Tube Ministry', it's about encountering a preacher on the underground, and 'sinning', as Sarah does when she sees Daphne,

> *I prove myself a sinner, allowing*
> *myself to scan with worldly eyes*
>
> *her shabby mack, her cheap red suit,*
> *that truly disastrous nylon blouse*
> *and to wonder, bitchily,*
> *if faith has deprived her of fashion sense.*

I do express sympathy for the preacher later in the poem, noting 'the humiliation shining in her cheeks', and wonder what motivates her, but, like Sarah, I am ashamed of having felt superior about this woman's clothes, and of having encountered the bitch in myself.

A snobby bitch, at that. The evangelical faith, the 'shabby mack' – does my preacher remind you of anyone? Mrs Woolf, were you ever ashamed of Miss Kilman?

Poor Doris Kilman: just as Daphne embodies a kind of

horror for Sarah, so she does for the titular character of your *Mrs Dalloway*. For not only does Clarissa Dalloway despise her daughter's history tutor for her lower-middle-class shabbiness, and feel inferior around her because of her university education, and resent her because her daughter Elizabeth has so much time for this other woman; she also abhors the emotions and thoughts that Miss Kilman's presence provokes in her own head. On the face of it, at least, Clarissa Dalloway is exactly the kind of woman that George must have wanted you and your sister to become: married to an important man, mistress of a fine establishment, beautiful, beautifully dressed, a perfect hostess, whose inner life, in polite company at least, remains quite perfectly unexpressed.

In short, Clarissa is a lady. However, she is a lady at the centre of a Virginia Woolf novel, and as such, her inner life must be laid bare: the guests at her party will never know her, but your readers will. I had read that Clarissa was based on an old family friend of yours, Kitty Maxse, née Lushington, but I did not realize – until I checked her details just now, to be honest – that she died three years before you published *Mrs Dalloway*. And a violent, premature death, too – a fall over the banisters in her house in South Kensington. It's so close to the suicide you wrote for Septimus Warren Smith in that same novel. I didn't know that you had contemplated giving this death to Clarissa, until you decided that the resemblance to Kitty's death would be too great. It isn't clear if Kitty's fall was accidental or deliberate, but you must have wondered. You certainly regretted that you had not seen her for so long, not since you were much younger, when she had tried to pressure you into marrying, and you 'cut' her for it.

Clarissa emerges, as all your characters do, from a nexus of complex, uncomfortable *lived-through* feelings. And that brings me back to Miss Kilman. When she is first described in Clarissa's stream of consciousness, it is disgust that brings her to mind, a disgusting smell, and a manky dog:

> Elizabeth really cared for her dog most of all. The whole house this morning smelled of tar. Still, better poor Grizzle than Miss Kilman; better distemper and tar and all the rest of it than sitting mewed in a stuffy bedroom with a prayer book![33]

Like Carrie and Daphne, Doris Kilman is one of those not-quite-females whose status as fully human appears to be up for debate, and Clarissa is both bewildered and mystified by her daughter's enthusiasm for this creature's company. As she contemplates the governess and her own dislike of her, she struggles to pin down what it is that she finds so appalling and her thoughts shift back and forth between self-justification and guilt. She knows she ought to distinguish between the trivial – the state of Miss Kilman's mackintosh – and the serious – the condition of her soul – but finds it impossible to separate them:

> and how she dressed, how she treated people who came to lunch she did not care a bit, it being her experience that the religious ecstasy made people callous (so did causes); dulled their feelings, for Miss Kilman would do anything for the Russians, starved herself for the Austrians, but in private inflicted positive torture, so insensitive was she, dressed in a green mackintosh coat. Year in year out she wore that coat; she perspired; she was never in the room five minutes without making you feel her superiority, your inferiority; how poor she was; how rich you were; how she lived in a slum without a cushion or a rug or a bed or

whatever it might be, all her soul rusted with that griev-
ance sticking in it, her dismissal during the War – poor,
embittered, unfortunate creature! For it was not her one
hated but the idea of her, which undoubtedly had gathered
to itself a great deal that was not Miss Kilman; had become
one of those spectres with which one battles in the night;
one of those spectres who stand astride us and suck up half
our life-blood, dominators and tyrants; for no doubt with
another throw of the dice, had the black been uppermost
and not the white, she would have loved Miss Kilman! But
not in this world. No.[34]

Or, as Sarah might put it, Doris Kilman reminds Clarissa
Dalloway of what a bitch she is, and Clarissa cannot forgive her
for it. I have also seen it said that she reminds us – and I'm sorry
to say it – of what a bitch Mrs Woolf could be. What was it you
said about Katherine Mansfield? Let me remind you: you said she
put you in mind of 'a civet cat that had taken to street-walking'.[35]
Katherine was your friend, but she could bring something ugly
out of you. In a way it is to your credit that we know this, in that
you were honest enough with yourself to recognize it and did
not censor it in your writings. Those extraordinary novels – *Mrs
Dalloway, To The Lighthouse, The Waves* – could never have come
about were it not for your pitiless commitment to the truth. It was
all part of your life's project, to find a language that can do justice
to women's inner lives, in all their complex unprettiness.

If all we ever read of Miss Kilman were Mrs Dalloway's
impressions of her, then it would be fair to say that she was
brought into being only to be the mirror for another character's
ugly insides, but there is more to Doris Kilman than that. We
never find out if Daphne knows what she represents for other

girls, let alone how she might feel about it, but your Miss Kilman is as much of a person as your Mrs Dalloway, and both characters are animated by their author's own felt experience. Both characters, for example, have something of your own love for and attraction to other women. There is a good deal of passionate love between women in *Mrs Dalloway*: Clarissa is preoccupied by memories of an intense girlhood friendship; Elizabeth reveres Miss Kilman; Miss Kilman is in love with Elizabeth. You might not have been able to speak of these experiences in public during your lifetime, but you are celebrated for them now. Your friend and lover Vita Sackville-West is recognized as the model for the gender-fluid protagonist of *Orlando*. They've made a film about your relationship with Vita. (Elizabeth Debicki plays you, and I'm glad to say she isn't sporting the ridiculous prosthetic nose that they stuck on Nicole Kidman's face for *The Hours*. What did they do that for? Did they think that a small pretty nose and troubled female genius were *ipso facto* incompatible? It didn't even look like your nose: far too wide all the way down, nothing like as elegant.)

You and Vita – was it partly the attraction of opposites? You suggest as much in an entry from your diary. It's 1925, and you have been marvelling at the glamorous figure Vita cuts, how she 'shone' even on a visit to a grocer's shop. Vita, on the other hand, 'found me incredibly dowdy, no woman cared less for personal appearance – no one put on things the way I did'.[36] When Vita had first encountered you three years earlier, she had described you to her husband as 'utterly unaffected: there are no outward adornments – she dresses quite atrociously. At first you think she is plain, then a sort of spiritual beauty imposes itself on you, and you find a fascination in watching her. She was smarter last night, that is to say, the woollen orange stockings were replaced by yellow silk ones, but she still wore the pumps.'[37] Vita may have been enthralled by you from the start, but that didn't mean that she could overlook your dress sense.

I'm sure it would have come as no surprise to Vita to discover that shopping for clothes made you so uncomfortable. You give Miss Kilman her own awkward shopping moment in *Mrs Dalloway*, when she visits the Army and Navy with Elizabeth, and it isn't too much of a stretch to read your own history of such moments in this scene: 'Elizabeth guided her this way and that; guided her in her abstraction as if she had been a great child, an unwieldy battleship… and she chose [a petticoat] in her abstraction, portentously, and the girl serving her thought her mad.'[38]

This image of Doris Kilman 'in her abstraction', appearing mad, reminds me of both of us. It reminds me of a lunch break in junior school, when I was sitting alone (as I usually was), thinking my thoughts and staring into the middle distance, when another girl walked up to me and informed me that I was mad. It reminds me of an incident in my early twenties, when I was walking back to my seat on a train, travelling alone and very much 'in my abstraction', and forgot to close a carriage door behind me – or perhaps it sprang open again – I don't remember which. What I do remember is that there was a group of teenagers sitting in the seats nearest the door. When I'm in my abstraction, I don't always register speech at first, especially if I'm not expecting anyone to speak to me, so the first I heard of their repeated requests was this, just behind my left ear: 'SHUT THE DOOR, YOU STUPID, STUCK-UP LITTLE COW!'

It also reminds me of your husband Leonard's description of you in your abstraction, and how people responded to you when you were in that state:

to the crowd in the street there was something in her appearance which struck them as strange and laughable… people would stare or stop and stare at Virginia. And not only in foreign towns; they would stop and stare and nudge one another – 'look at her' – even in England, in Piccadilly or Lewes.[39]

In these moments, it was your manner, even more than your clothes, that marked you out as different. Because when a woman like you or me or Miss Kilman is in her abstraction, her manner marks her out as a woman who moves through the world as if the way she appears to the other people in it were not her primary concern. And there's a price to be paid for that. When those boys shouted 'Dog!' at me, I'm sure that it was my abstracted expression, my lack of self-consciousness in the face of their gaze, and the way I carelessly returned it that offended, quite as much as my careless appearance. A woman is not supposed to forget – not even for a moment – that whatever else she is, she is also an object.

And now we're back to the moment when you offended your half-brother George, because you had neglected the obligation to check yourself in the internalized mirror of the male gaze. If you'd prefer a formulation from phenomenology rather than film theory, I can offer you one from Iris Marion Young's essay 'Throwing Like a Girl', in which she explains that to become a woman is to develop a double sense of oneself, as a subject in the world but also as an object 'to be gazed at and decorated'.[40] As Young reminds her readers, such an object is by definition 'vulnerable'. A subject does; an object is done to. As you revealed in your unpublished autobiographical writings, those humiliating evenings that began with George's assessing your person as if it were so much horse flesh usually ended with his walking into your bedroom and sexually assaulting you.

But here I'm mostly talking about those other harms, the smaller humiliations which become so powerful in the accumulation. You have to have experienced them to understand how much they hurt. I have experienced the kinds of adverse events in my life – physical illnesses, traumatic losses, a difficult labour – that freely elicit everyone's sympathy, but if I were to be honest about it, I would have to say that these experiences, for the most part, are not the hardest to live with. And if they are not the hardest, it is precisely *because* they elicit sympathy. The more easily people can imagine themselves in your place, the more easily and wholeheartedly they can sympathize.

Those other experiences, the ones that seem so trivial but sting so much, are characterized by humiliation, and the social rejection that comes with it. Think back to Carrie in the shower, her ungroomed, pimpled body on display, bleeding and wailing like an animal. Sue Snell can see that Carrie is in pain, but she knows better than to show it, because Carrie is, in that moment, the very embodiment of all that is abject and shameful, of all the truths about our shared animal vulnerability that we spend so much time and money and energy to deny, and this makes her dangerous to approach. So Sue keeps her distance, both physical and emotional, while the other girls go on the attack, pointing, laughing and pelting Carrie with sanitary products, objects that in themselves are never supposed to be seen. (Oh, the embarrassment when one of them falls out of a handbag, even with its pretty floral wrapping intact!) People move to comfort grief; they shun humiliation.

It is extraordinarily painful to enter into the experience of a shamed character, a character on the receiving end of laughter.

A writer would have to have a very good reason for doing so; in your case, I think it must have been your absolute determination to find the language to describe hidden experience, no matter how ugly it was. Often experiences remain undescribed simply because they are taken for granted or disregarded, but sometimes it is because, like Carrie in the shower, they are pulsing all through with a shame that makes them dangerous to approach. Sarah can barely bring herself to speculate about Daphne's inner life: the thought that Daphne might *know* that she is Daphne is almost too horrible to contemplate. But you leave your readers in no doubt that Miss Kilman knows what she represents to Clarissa Dalloway. You give Doris Kilman a feeling, thinking inner life. When Carrie is laughed at, the reader is with Sue Snell, witnessing the humiliation from a safe distance; when Clarissa Dalloway laughs at Miss Kilman, the narrative shifts abruptly from Clarissa's perspective to Doris's, and the full depth of her humiliation is there for the reader to feel and experience:

> It was the flesh she must control. Clarissa Dalloway had insulted her. That she expected. But she had not triumphed; she had not mastered the flesh. Ugly, clumsy, Clarissa Dalloway had laughed at her for being that; and had revived the fleshly desires, for she minded looking as she did beside Clarissa. Nor could she talk as she did. But why wish to resemble her? Why? She despised Mrs Dalloway from the bottom of her heart. She was not serious. She was not good. Her life was a tissue of vanity and deceit. Yet Doris Kilman had been overcome. She had, as a matter of fact, very nearly burst into tears when Clarissa Dalloway laughed at her. 'It is the flesh, it is the flesh,' she muttered (it being her habit to talk aloud), trying to subdue this turbulent and painful

feeling as she walked down Victoria Street. She prayed to God. She could not help being ugly; she could not afford to buy pretty clothes. Clarissa Dalloway had laughed – but she would concentrate her mind upon something else until she had reached the pillar-box. At any rate she had got Elizabeth. But she would think of something else; she would think of Russia; until she reached the pillar-box.

How nice it must be, she said, in the country, struggling, as Mr Whittaker had told her, with that violent grudge against the world which had scorned her, sneered at her, cast her off, beginning with this indignity – the infliction of her unlovable body which people could not bear to see. Do her hair as she might, her forehead remained like an egg, bald, white. No clothes suited her. She might buy anything. And for a woman, of course, that meant never meeting the opposite sex. Never would she come first with any one.[41]

Of course you were beautiful, you were able – sometimes – to find clothes that suited you, you did know what it was to come first with someone, but I do believe that through Miss Kilman you were able to give expression to a state of being that you knew all too well. Part of that state is the shame of allowing oneself to feel utterly destroyed by something that we are told is trivial. Miss Kilman knows, as you knew, and as I know, that no woman worth taking seriously is supposed to care what other people think she looks like. Doris Kilman despises Clarissa Dalloway and all her accomplishments, but her laughter feels close to annihilating. When I read Leonard's account of the 'crowd in the street' mocking you, I thought immediately of a sentence in your earlier novel, *Jacob's Room*, and how much I recognized the truth of it:

It's not catastrophes, murders, deaths, diseases, that age and kill us; it's the way people look and laugh, and run up the steps of omnibuses.[42]

I have been thinking through that sentence of yours ever since I first read it. I took it as the epigraph of the first chapter of my first book. If I have been able to speak my shame, it is only because you were brave enough to speak first. Since you died, Mrs Woolf, you have become the guarantor of other women's truth. As I said at the beginning of my letter, you have been working exceptionally hard.

You'll remember that I also said that I had some further work in mind for you, that I wished you to represent something you had not been called on to represent before. You'll notice that I have held back from naming it so far. It is not something that most readers would recognize in you, or wish to recognize. It's a stigmatized identity, a medicalized one – a condition, in other words; the people who possess it are assumed to be deficient in imagination and interpersonal intelligence, and to lack the capacity to exercise their full adult agency. It would be bad enough to imply all that about someone I'd never even met, but to imply it about someone of your exceptional talent and accomplishment is considered to be far worse. This is because of the paradoxical nature of this condition in the public mind: while it is associated with severe deficiency, it is also associated with exceptional talent and accomplishment, in such a way that the talents and accomplishments of the person concerned are often unjustly attributed to the condition instead of the person. The concept I'm circling around had yet to be formulated in your lifetime, but any modern reader will have guessed it by now and must be urging me under their breath to just come out with it. OK, then: it's autism. I'm talking about autism.

—and with that word I find myself back where I started, loitering on the threshold of a room I'm not sure I should enter, carrying an unasked-for gift that might well be distasteful to the recipient. George brought you an ugly jewel and interrupted your Greek. I don't want to risk being like George, pushing myself into your space, insisting that you perform a role I've foisted on you for my own ends. So let me make one thing absolutely clear: I am not diagnosing you with anything – not only because I shouldn't but also because I can't. In order to diagnose you, I would have to be a qualified psychologist, you would have to be alive and we would have to be present at the same time in the same room. So you and the many living people whom a diagnosis would offend can be reassured that a diagnosis is in no danger of happening.

What I'm edging towards is not a diagnosis of Virginia Woolf the late person but a way of reading the life and work of Virginia Woolf as she lives in the surviving texts. I hope you would agree that when we read a text or a life in a new way, or from a novel position, it enables us to see all those patterns of meaning and experience that might never have showed themselves before; that in doing so we can enrich our understanding of that life, the position from which we read it, and the relationship between the two. The path to my own autism diagnosis began with my reading of other lives, when I recognized myself in the autobiographies of autistic women. Donna Williams, Rudy Simone, Dawn Prince-Hughes and Liane Holliday Willey were the mothers I had to think through in order to come to that new understanding of myself. After I was diagnosed, I was able to view my life history through that lens, and so many moments that up till then had hurt me in part precisely because I could make no sense of them immediately lost a little of their sting. They lost a little more because I also realized that other people had experienced the same kinds of painful moments and for the same reasons. For the first time, I could be sure that there were some rooms I could enter where my experiences were comprehensible, where I didn't have to apologize, offer a tortuous explanation of myself or turn myself into a joke.

Not all that many rooms, though. Autistic culture is a minority culture, and there are certain kinds of work that minority cultures need to do if they are to have any chance of thriving: they need to establish their right to exist and to define themselves; they need to carve out and protect their own spaces; they need to recover a version of their history that is their own, that has not been imposed upon them. Autism as a distinct diagnosis came into being in the forties, when a US-based psychiatrist called Leo Kanner identified certain patterns of behaviour in a group of children at his clinic. I could never quite recognize myself in his version of autism, or in the current clinical versions that are descended from it. That's because they are describing autism from the outside, as a set of symptoms or deficits, a set of distinct ways of failing to be normal. Autism from the inside, as a way of experiencing and navigating and making sense of the world, autism as a particular way of being – that I've known all my life; that I have no trouble owning. But generally, when you say the word 'autism' to people, what they think you have told them is that you have sat the Normality Exam and failed – and you have, multiple times, every time you entered a room or occupied it incorrectly; every time you dressed and groomed yourself incorrectly; every time you held your female body or moved it incorrectly, or spoke incorrectly or laughed incorrectly or did the wrong thing with your face. The shame, the sting of all those moments isn't lessened by describing them in clinical terms; they just acquire a medical smell. Psychologists and psychiatrists sometimes like to argue that their language is value-neutral, but I don't believe that language which people use to describe other people could ever be.

The American legal commentator Jeffrey Rosen once observed that 'there are few acts more aggressive than describing someone else'.[43] When we describe another person, we act as a subject and make of that other person an object. You understood this very well. I'm thinking about that section in *A Room of One's Own* where you survey centuries of literature by men in which they described women from the outside, as if womanhood were a disorder with its characteristic set of symptoms and deficits, a set of ways of failing to be male. For all that time, womanhood from the inside, as a way of experiencing and navigating and making sense of the world, was expressed, for the most part, only in unpublished words, in letters and private journals. Those few women who dared to write for publication did so without approval, without formal education, without recourse to established tradition. As you tell it, these brave women struggled on the page, as they tried to negotiate between the felt pressure of their own perceptions and experiences and the established forms of language which resisted their attempts to express them. Once they published, their works were condemned and belittled, then, after their deaths, forgotten. The effect of this was that every time another woman sat down to write, she did so believing she was alone, with no mothers to think through. She could not hope to write with the sense of entitlement, the confidence you saw in those legions of male writers who described women. And you perceived a strong link between them, between these acts of description and the confidence with which they were committed:

Life for both sexes... is arduous, difficult, a perpetual struggle. It calls for gigantic courage and strength. More than anything, perhaps, creatures of illusion as we are, it calls for confidence in oneself. Without self-confidence we are as babes in the cradle. And how can we generate this imponderable quality, which is yet so invaluable, most quickly? By thinking that other people are inferior to oneself. By thinking that one has some innate superiority – it may be wealth, or rank, a straight nose, the portrait of a grandfather by Romney – for there is no end to the pathetic devices of the human imagination – over other people.[44]

When I was small, I wanted to be a boy. No, it was more than that – I thought that I had to *be* a boy. I understand that there are children who refuse to identify with the sex on their birth certificate because they are trans, but I've never thought that was the case with me. It was more that the assumption everywhere, in the early seventies, seemed to be that women were lesser beings than men, and girls lesser beings than boys, that they did lesser things and lived lesser lives, and I did not see why I should accept those lesser conditions. There was a whole world out there for me to observe and explore and think about, and I had no interest in interrupting my activities so that the world could look at me and judge whether I was pretty or nice or good – whether, in other words, I was becoming a girl. Why on earth would I want to be one of *those*? Why would I, when I was so much more interested in looking than in being looked at? Why should I accept that the purpose of my existence was, as you put it in *A Room of One's Own*, to serve as a looking glass 'possessing the magic and delicious power of reflecting the figure of man at twice its natural size'?[45]

As you say, men have long been able to think themselves superior to women. People of European extraction have been able to believe ourselves possessed of a quality called 'whiteness' which renders us superior to those who do not have it. Heterosexual people have been able to regard homosexual people as defective, 'inverted' versions of ourselves. In every case, one class has for the longest time reserved to itself the privilege of describing and defining the other. The same goes for able-bodied people and disabled people. For hearing and D/deaf people. And, as long as the categories have existed, for non-autistic and autistic people.

Not long after I was diagnosed, I embarked on a PhD, and – thinking that it was the proper thing to do – I applied for Disabled Students' Allowance. The assessor was thrown by me. Very early on, he pointed out how different I was from his other autistic clients: I made eye contact; my answers were relevant to his questions. He wondered how a student with Asperger's Syndrome could manage a PhD in Creative Writing. He said that he would have expected someone with my clinical profile (looking from my file to me and back again) to have dropped out of my first degree, which I hadn't. I had naively thought that my diagnosis was all the evidence I needed to obtain the assistance I was asking for – I hadn't realized that I had to perform the role of someone with that diagnosis. I hadn't realized that this role necessitated that I display some kind of perceptible inferiority to my assessor. I had often failed at being a woman. Now, apparently, I was failing to be autistic. I was also – let's not forget – talking to a man who wanted to keep control of his interaction with a woman. We are all occupying multiple roles at any given time, and these roles inflect each other.

Yesterday I was re-reading Hermione Lee's biography of you, specifically the chapter in which she examines the crises of physical and mental health that recurred throughout your life. She shows how much your understanding of the ways in which you were oppressed as a woman was bound up with your experience of oppression as a patient. The roles inflected each other, but in *Mrs Dalloway* you chose to give your experience of this particular kind of oppression to a male character: Septimus Warren Smith, the shell-shocked returning soldier. Septimus's doctors are insensitive brutes. His GP, Dr Holmes, insists that there is 'nothing whatever the matter'.[46] 'he brushed it all aside – headaches, sleeplessness, fears, dreams – nerve symptoms and nothing more, he said.'[47] He sits by Septimus's bed and tries to jolly him out of his 'funk' with a reminder of his duty to his wife and a suggestion that he take up some hobby. Holmes reminds me a little of my own family GP, who knew me before I was even born, who vaccinated me, dosed me, referred me sometimes, watched me grow up, and then, when I asked for help with depression in my early twenties, told me that I thought too much and that an attractive girl like me only needed to go out, have fun and find a boyfriend. Nothing the matter with either of us: Septimus only needs to act like a man, I only needed to act like a girl, and all would be right as rain. To perform the role of a sane person is to perform one's gender role correctly.

I did not take my GP's advice. A few years later, my father died and another doctor, an elderly male locum who wanted to get a weeping girl out of his consulting room, prescribed me fluoxetine, a selective serotonin reuptake inhibitor (SSRI) commonly known as Prozac. I'm not sorry he did. SSRIs work for me: they keep my various anxieties at bay and help me to write. In 2019, I think I can say that there are some psychiatric treatments available that work sometimes for some people. But for you and Septimus, there was nothing on offer for your 'nerves' but bromide, forced inactivity and supervised overfeeding. In the novel, Septimus's wife takes him to see a Harley Street specialist, Sir William Bradshaw, who declares that Septimus must have complete rest in one of Sir

William's homes, 'rest in bed; rest in solitude; silence and rest; rest without friends, without books, without messages; six months' rest',[48] until he is fattened up and healthy again. Rest and fattening – this was your treatment. George Savage, who oversaw your care after breakdowns in your twenties and thirties, is often taken to be the model for the overbearing Bradshaw.

In *Mrs Dalloway*, nobody seems to have any interest in or respect for Septimus's own experience of his condition, his traumatic memories or his survivor's guilt. Nobody seems to have had all that much respect for yours, either. Lee quotes from your doctor's reports, from your husband's observations and your sister's letters – they all focus on your behaviour and what might be done to amend it. There is no sense that anyone is listening to your distress. When you are ill, they do not let you write.

Perhaps if you were living now, you might have chosen to write publicly about your experiences of mental illness. Since your time, psychiatric patients have learned to organize as a group, to speak together and to get their experiential knowledge into mainstream discourse and culture: members of patient groups are invited to participate in the design of research studies, consulted on policy, and sometimes employed as 'experts by experience'. This is all very positive, of course, but it doesn't change the unequal power relationship between those who use services and those who provide them, or between those who identify as being a certain kind of person and those who formulate the official definition of what such a person is. Professionals – clinicians, researchers, educators – maintain their authority over what counts as knowledge about a condition.

Autism, though not a mental illness as such, remains the province of psychologists and psychiatrists. Autistic people have begun to organize and speak on our own behalf, but we are rarely heard. And when we are, the context in which our utterances are framed and interpreted is almost always determined by the non-autistic: non-autistic autism professionals, the non-autistic parents of autistic people, voluntary organizations run by non-autistic people and, in the media, by non-autistic journalists, editors and producers. By people whose first question is not 'How do you experience your world?' but 'How might we recognize you in ours?' (In what way are you autistic? How did they diagnose you? You don't seem autistic at all.)

When I first read your work, I did not identify as autistic, but I did identify with you. As I read your novels and essays, and later your autobiographical writings, I felt understood and less alone. I could think through them, as I would later think through the writing of women who did identify as autistic. At this moment I'm picturing you as a girl once again, unwillingly crossing thresholds on George's arm, attempting to wear the wrong dress, failing to act like a girl, and the very particular nature and texture of your failure feels so familiar to me. You write that you had previously enjoyed a dance in Cambridge, with your brother Thoby's friends, and did not expect the London ones to be too onerous, but one night out with George was enough to make you understand why Vanessa had found them so detestable:

> After two hours of standing about in Lady Sligo's ball-room, of waiting to be introduced to strange young men, of dancing a round with Conrad Russell or with Esme Howard, of dancing very badly, of being left without a partner, of being told by George that I looked lovely but must hold myself upright, I retired to an ante-room and hoped that a curtain concealed me.[49]

I once went to a dance at school, in the sixth form. The boys had been bussed in from their own single-sex private establishment and most of the other girls were wearing Laura Ashley. I had no prior acquaintance with any of the boys, wore a long, tight Morticia Addams crushed velvet black dress from Richard Shops, and danced with nobody. I went to one May Ball during my time at Cambridge, in a group but without a partner. Most of the other girls were wearing strapless, straight-skirted ball gowns; I wore a full-skirted vintage fifties dress from Camden Market. My group quickly split into its constituent pairs, and I spent most of the night wandering about on my own. I could have done with an ante-room, especially as it was raining so hard.

At Lady Sligo's dance you had disappointed George by being too subdued. But, as it turned out, when you were animated, you were animated in the wrong way. A few days after the miserable dance, you accompanied him to dinner with the Dowager Countess of Carnarvon and her sister, Mrs Popham. George 'had always complained of Vanessa's silence', so you were keen to show that you could talk. Encouraged by the ladies' 'mild and kindly' conversation, you write that you 'soon felt that I could not only reply to their questions... but initiate remarks of my own'. As your confidence took hold, you began to hold forth:

> Heaven knows what devil prompted me – or why to Lady Carnarvon and Mrs Popham of Littlecote of all people in the world I, a chit of eighteen, should have chosen to discourse upon the need of expressing the emotions! That, I said, was the great lack of modern life. The ancients, I said, discussed everything in common. Had Lady Carnarvon ever read the dialogues of Plato? 'We – both men and women – ' once launched it was difficult to stop, nor was I sure that my

audacity was not holding them spellbound with admiration. I felt that I was earning George's gratitude forever. Suddenly a twitch, a shiver, a convulsion of amazing expressiveness, shook the Countess by my side; her diamonds, of which she wore a chaste selection, flashed in my eyes; and stopping, I saw George Duckworth blushing crimson on the other side of the table. I realised that I had committed some unspeakable impropriety. Lady Carnarvon and Mrs Popham began at once to talk of something entirely different; and directly dinner was over George, pretending to help me on with my cloak, whispered in my ear in a voice of agony, 'They're not used to young women saying anything –.'[50]

Of course it was not the fact that you spoke that was offensive, so much as what you spoke about (men and women and emotions) and the way you spoke about it (intensely, fiercely, displaying your unwomanly intellect). The Countess displayed her breeding by wearing only a 'chaste selection' of her diamonds, and you ought to have displayed only so much of your intelligence as was becoming to a young woman just out. And not have mentioned anything even adjacent to sex. Just as when I was at a garden party when I was fourteen I should not have held forth on George Orwell's *1984* and his use of the word 'orgasm' in relation to the frenzy at Oceania's political rallies.

Over time, I learned to adjust my behaviour as I had learned to adjust my dress and attend to my grooming. As a result, I began to fail fewer normality exams. The effort cost me hugely, and the best I could manage, for the most part, was a very mediocre pass. Each time I would feel momentary relief and a small sense of achievement, only for it to evaporate as I scrutinized my performance and took note of all my mistakes. I did not feel good about myself after these occasions. It is hard to feel triumphant about scraping through when so many other people seem to make so much less of an effort and do so much better. Especially once it has dawned on you that no amount of effort on your part will ever enable you to catch up.

You learned too, when you had to. In 'A Sketch of the Past' you describe how you and Vanessa, bowing to the 'pressure of society', acquired that '"manner" which we both still use', and would use it to receive guests, first with your father and later with George, at home in Hyde Park Gate. The manner comprised, as you acknowledged, a handy social skill-set:

> We both learned the rules of the Victorian game of manners so thoroughly that we have never forgotten them. We still play the game. It is useful; it has its beauty, for it is founded upon restraint, sympathy, unselfishness – all civilised qualities. It is helpful in making something seemly and human out of raw odds and ends.[51]

And so you learned to take your own 'odds and ends' and re-arrange them so that you could pass as a Victorian lady. More than that – to some extent, you *became* that nice Victorian lady. To the same extent, I *am* that nice, middle-class, middle-aged white cis-het woman – the kind of woman whom specialists describe in their letters to GPs as a 'pleasant lady' (and it is as one well-drilled pleasant lady to another that I take care to address you always as 'Mrs Woolf'). As Simone de Beauvoir said, a woman is 'made not born', and we both yielded, as much as our natures allowed, to the pressure to make ourselves over.

It has often been suggested, not by the way, that autistic women are diagnosed later than men because we are so good at 'masking' or 'camouflaging' our autism. Maybe this is something innate in us; maybe it is because the pressure of society is exerted so much more strongly and minutely on girls than it is on boys. Did you ever hear of a boy's being told he ought to re-arrange his legs when sitting down? Being ordered to smile in the street by a complete stranger? Being called a dog for leaving the house without make-up on? Would a head teacher stand up in the assembly hall of a boys' school at Christmas and tell the student body to make sure it listened to its old aunts' stories and laughed at its uncles' awful jokes? Sometimes I wonder if all women – autistic or otherwise – are not in fact 'masking' or 'camouflaging' or suppressing some very large part of themselves. I think you wondered the very same thing. It takes a huge amount of effort and attention to be Mrs Dalloway.

We are, all of us, striving constantly to pass those normality exams, to take our raw and boundless selves and squash them into the forms of neater girls and nicer women. The likes of Carrie and Daphne and Miss Kilman are there to warn us that the world will not be kind to us if we do not. Don't let your unsightly hair protrude from your hosiery; don't let your intimidating knowledge spurt out of your mouth. We keep to these rules in the hope that doing so will prevent those shameful moments I've been examining (and they might); we keep to them as if we accepted the implicit promise that to do so will keep us safe, as if we believed that bad things never happened to nice girls (although everyone knows, deep down, that they do).

It doesn't only come at a price, this squashing – it is its own price. You acknowledge the usefulness of the Victorian 'manner', but you go on to suggest that it is 'perhaps – I am not sure – a disadvantage in writing'.[52] You look at your earlier *Common Reader* articles and wonder if they were perhaps not too polite. By the

time you came to write 'A Sketch of the Past', you were survey-
ing that Victorian persona from a great distance: it was 1939 or
perhaps 1940; you were no longer an untried young girl but a distinguished, celebrated older writer; you were writing for yourself,
not looking for approval, trying to work out the truth of your own
nature and upbringing and their relation to your writing, and you
were determined to hold nothing back. You wrote of your losses.
Your fears and your horrors. Your feelings of unladylike resent-
ment towards your upbringing, your parents and George. Your
joys, of which there were so very many, and so many that would
be inaccessible to the Georges and Lady Carnarvons of this world,
who see everything only in terms of its practical or social use, and
never stop to delight in the beauty or rightness of things in themselves. As you did. As I hope I do. As autistic people, with that way
of loving people and ideas and things regardless of their social or
practical value, do and always will do.

I am so grateful to you for everything you wrote, but I have a
special fondness for those late autobiographical writings, for '22
Hyde Park Gate' and 'A Sketch of the Past', where you examined your girlhood – and the failures of your girlhood – holding
nothing back. If you had not described these awkward moments
and unpretty feelings, I might never have recognized my own in
them; if I had not had you to think through, I might never have
been able to think about myself, honestly or truthfully, at all. I
might never have been able to bear the shame. So, even though
you may never have wished me to see these writings, I hope you
will accept my gratitude for them. And I hope you will accept my
gratitude for helping me to think about those parts of myself and
my experience that I have come to understand as autistic. Or – to
use a word that was in use in your lifetime – weird. That awkward
part of myself that stumbles as it enters a room; that boundless

self that can come across a bolt of cloth in an upholstery department and see at once that there is no reason – no reason worth
considering at least – why it should not make a beautiful dress.
Thank you for showing me how to think through our mothers,
and through our sisters too.

Thank you, most weird Mrs Woolf.

Yours in sisterhood,
Dr Joanne Limburg

Adelheid Bloch

Adelheid Bloch (12 April 1908–25 June 1940) was born in Konstanz in the Baden-Württemberg region of Germany, the daughter of Moritz Bloch and his second wife, Ida. She was named in memory of her father's first wife, Adele. The Bloch family were prominent members of the Jewish community in Konstanz. When Adelheid was three, she contracted meningitis (or 'encephalitis', depending on which version of her life you consult), which left her with permanent brain damage. In June 1927, when she was nineteen years old, she was taken to a psychiatric hospital at Wiesloch, where she lived for the rest of her short life. After the Nazis came to power, the focus of activities at Wiesloch changed, as it did at other facilities of its kind, from care to eugenic research. As a disabled person, Adelheid was now seen as a 'useless eater', a burden on the Reich, and a problem to be solved. The solution to the existence of people like Adelheid came with 'Aktion T4', a deliberately uninformative label for a programme of systematic mass murder, initially of disabled children, which was rolled out to include disabled adults. On 25 June 1940, Adelheid was taken to the new killing centre at Grafeneck, where she was gassed, and her body cremated. Disabled people were the first group to be subject to this treatment. There is a memorial to Adelheid, a

Stolperstein or 'stumbling stone', set into the pavement outside what was the Bloch family home. One member of her family, Dr Erich Bloch, did return to Konstanz after the war, where he established a Jewish library. Some other members of the extended family also survived, and moved to Israel. One of their descendants is named as the 'godfather' of her *Stolperstein*.

Letter to Adelheid Bloch

Dear Adelheid

I have a confession to make – I almost didn't write to you.

When I began trying to figure out where my weird sisters might have lived, the first places that came to mind were institutions: convents, reform schools, workhouses, prisons and, of course, lunatic asylums. So the first place I looked was the asylum nearest to home. I went to the local records office, and had a leaf through the admissions book of what was, in the nineteenth and early twentieth centuries, the Isle of Ely and Borough of Cambridge Asylum. Most entries had only one word in the column marked for diagnosis: 'mania' or 'dementia', the first meaning, roughly, 'mood disorder', and the second, 'psychosis'. There were occasional notes about how the patients got to their unfortunate state: bereavement, a violent husband and in one case 'political overexcitement'. I had imagined people were put away forever, but in fact most patients stayed only for a few months. The exceptions, the long-stayers who never got out, were usually distinguished by the presence of another word in the diagnosis column, that word being 'imbecile'.

The difference was brutally stark: mad people could go home to their families, but imbeciles belonged to the institution. As did 'idiots', 'morons', the 'feeble-minded' and 'mental defectives' – as the nineteenth century turned into the twentieth, the terminology changed, but the tone remained: dismissive, detached and clinical. People with these labels – people like you – were not people, but problems for people to solve. The way the problem was framed, and the proposed solutions, changed as the terminology changed, but not in your favour.

I found you in an article by the sociologist Lutz Kaelber, entitled 'Jewish Children with Disabilities and Nazi "Euthanasia" Crimes'. Naming you as 'Adelheid B', he cites your case as an instance of the way in which 'more radical views toward Jews with disabilities and mental illnesses came to the fore [in Germany] at the same time.'[53] Female, mentally ill, disabled, Jewish – four shared boxes ticked. As a Jew brought up in the seventies and eighties, I was given to understand that I had a duty to bear witness to the Holocaust, to remember, to make sure that your memories and names would never be erased as your living bodies and minds had been. You and I have Jewishness in common, and for that reason alone, I would always place us together, I would always acknowledge us as us.

Sometimes I tell people that moving through society as a Jew for fifty years has been the perfect preparation for learning to move through society as a late-diagnosed autistic person: in both cases, you disclose the fact, and then the person you've disclosed it to gets to have fun deciding whether you look it or not. In both cases, it comes down to passing, and passing privilege. I don't always have it. People who've grown up among Jews can clock me pretty quickly – although my features are not stereotypical, I share them with a lot of other European Jews; and then there's my accent, which my non-Jewish husband once described as 'North London Non-Specific Ethnic'.

The autism's another matter. I've written elsewhere that people often sense something different about me, but they rarely identify the source of the difference, unless I disclose it. If I'm not like the autistic individuals they live with, or work with, or have seen on television, they struggle to see what it is that's autistic about me. The assumption is, always, that there must be something to see – something that would signal my deficiency. I'm what people insist on calling 'high-functioning', which means that I can make my appearance conform to theirs when I have to, I can behave as they expect a woman to behave, I can use spoken language in a way they can understand – I can pass.

You could not. According to your records, you were diagnosed with 'idiocy' and your physician described you as 'terribly difficult and disruptive'. Kaelber speculates that you had 'a developmental disability – according to a local historian trained as a psychotherapist with access to her records, [Adelheid] may in fact have had autism, which did not exist as a diagnostic category at the time'.[54] I wrote to Kaelber to ask about his source, and he directed me to the historian Dr Frank Janzowski. Dr Janzowski told me that when you were three, you contracted meningitis (sometimes translated as 'encephalitis'), which left you brain-damaged. Yes, you presented in a very similar way to the children Leo Kanner would name 'autistic' a few years later, but in your case, there was an identifiable organic cause. And it is also worth mentioning that, when you arrived at Wiesloch in the twenties, you were not a child.

Adelheid, it was at this point that I nearly abandoned you. I allowed myself to think for a moment that you fell outside the scope of this project. But then I realized that in judging you to be outside the scope of things, to be too unlike me to be claimed as one of mine, I was guilty of doing what others had done to you. Of being dismissive, detached and clinical, little better than the physician who described you as more like an animal than a person, and noted that, when ill, you showed no signs of feeling pain.

Maybe you did, though – maybe you did, and he just lacked the sensitivity and the imagination to read them. How the hell could he tell what pain you suffered? Nobody can really judge what goes on in another person's head, nobody can know for sure how much another person understands, what they feel, how joyful or painful or rich their experience of being alive might be. I don't know for sure whether you can understand this letter, but I'll do you the courtesy of 'assuming capacity', and write to you as one person to another. Even if you cannot understand this letter, it is no less yours – a gift is still a gift, even if you can't find a use for it. I would never claim to speak for you, but I can, and will, speak *to* you. And I still owe you an apology, whether you can understand the words or not.

There's something else important we have in common, besides our Jewishness. I can pass now, but I wasn't always able to, and, like you, I know what it is to be seen as a problem in need of a solution. When I was growing up, I kept being asked the same two questions, again and again:

What is the matter with you?

What are we going to do with you?

I used to wonder why people kept asking me these questions. They obviously didn't want or expect me to answer.

What is the matter with you?

You can't speak or you can't speak properly.

From what I know of you, I assume that you had little or no speech – that your 'expressive language skills', as they are sometimes called, were non-existent or at best very limited. I'm guessing from the use of the word 'idiocy' that your difficulty in expressing thoughts in spoken language was taken as evidence of a lack of both language comprehension and of any thoughts worth expressing. People who regard themselves as normal often make these kinds of assumptions about people who struggle with speech, whatever the reason for their struggles might be.

Autism is routinely described as something a person can have 'mildly' or 'severely'. Problems with expressive language are often cited as proof of 'severity', and this severity is assumed to include an element of intellectual disability. In this way, the mild/severe distinction is taken to indicate not only a difference in degree but a difference in kind: someone like me – so 'eloquent', so 'articulate' – can't possibly 'suffer' from the same 'condition' as a non-speaker.

But it's really not as simple as that. For a start, there are quite a few autistic people who can write but not speak, and it is not because they have no thoughts to express, but because, as Daniel McConnell puts it, 'my mind moves like lightening and my body like a cement truck';[55] autistic bodies can be very, very heavy steering, and this can affect the motor planning and physical coordination required for speech, or, in many cases, unassisted typing. And a couple more things to remember: first of all, not all thoughts are made of words; secondly, when you are autistic, and your experiences are so different from most people's, you are often speaking in translation, even when the language is supposedly your own.

And sometimes you're just too scared to speak.

When I was eight, and had recently moved from the Infants to the Juniors, it became apparent to my parents that there was something off-kilter about me. It was becoming apparent to the other children too. From time to time, one of my classmates would look at me, head on one side, eyes narrowed, and offer their version of a diagnosis: 'You have a stammer, don't you?' One girl told me, with some excitement and a great deal of pride in her knowledge, that it was a sort of handicap. I can remember where we were standing when she said it, but I can't remember what my response was. Only that I can't have been looking her in the face, because my visual memory of the moment is filled entirely with the sky and the playing field and the fence that went all the way around it.

What are we going to do with you?
I was taken to a speech therapist, who noticed, among other things, this habit of not looking people in the face. I have a copy of the letter she sent to the paediatrician. It begins:

> Joanne presents as an extremely bright particularly verbally, insightful and shy girl.

[We'll come back to this – for now, note the word 'shy'.]

> At the first interview she was completely fluent. It was only in the middle of the second session, that Joanne demonstrated hesitancy, initial sound, and syllable repetitions, and very occasionally mild initial sound blocks. She severely lacked eye contact, and on a number of occasions turned her head to one side.

[I still do that sometimes, by the way; it's not always easy to organize my thoughts and cope with the stimulus of an attentive

human face at one and the same time, and clinicians tend to dem-
onstrate higher than average attentiveness in their gaze.]

> For a girl of Joanne's age she is extremely aware in a precise
> way in which people and situations cause her stammer to
> develop from a very mild dysfluency to what she consid-
> ers as a moderately severe dysfluency (that is, whole word
> repetition).

[The self-consciousness hasn't gone away either. The surprise for
me here is how early it kicked in.]

> The dysfluency is very fluctuating. Neither her class
> teacher, nor her headmaster, with whom I have spoken at
> some length have ever detected even the mildest stammer.

[One-to-ones with adults – a teacher or a speech therapist – were
never the hardest interactions for me. However, things did dete-
riorate with the headmaster. We'll come back to that too.]

> Joanne's feelings towards her stammer include embarrass-
> ment and anger. Joanne is over-conscious of her speech,
> in general, and very aware when she makes a 'slip of
> the tongue'. She responds by stumbling and the form
> the stammer takes will then depend on the person(s) or
> situation.
> According to her the situations which cause most
> dysfluency are where a demand is made or giving an
> accurate verbal account before a group or reading orally
> in class.

[It depends on the situation and the group: an audience who've come to see me read are genuinely well disposed towards me and I've usually had some quiet time beforehand; when I'm in front of a class of restless late adolescents at three in the afternoon, with a dayful of interactions behind me, words will sometimes literally fail me. The wrong ones will come out, or the right ones in the wrong order, or they will cut out altogether. Sometimes I will have a picture of the thing I want to talk about, but not the word, and will have to resort to improvised sign language to prompt myself – unfortunately for me, I seem to look funny when I do that.

This makes teaching difficult – not impossible by any means, but difficult. I've learned to cope by keeping whole-class inter-actions down to a minimum, and always having visual prompts in front of me, so that I can cut down the amount of time I have to spend looking into a roomful of faces which might have frighten-ing expressions on them – any hint of disapproval or mockery or incomprehension and something inside me seizes up with fear.

Debating is impossible, though only when the subject is some-thing I care about. I discovered this in the most humiliating way when I was fifteen, and had decided to improvise my speech in front of the class opposing the motion that a woman's place was in the home. I stopped dead halfway through an impassioned sen-tence. My limbic brain had got itself all worked up and throttled whatever bits of my cerebral cortex were involved with speech and language use. It was just like unexpectedly walking bang into a plate-glass window, and as I have also done that I can tell you that it was every bit as embarrassing. Yes, I definitely felt embarrass-ment and anger on that occasion.]

Four months later, after a few more sessions, the therapist wrote that I was feeling less 'frightened', was better able to cope when people 'commented adversely' on my stammer, and that everyone agreed I could be discharged.

I speak – a lot, usually fluently, and sometimes professionally – but that doesn't mean I don't still struggle with speech. I struggle in all kinds of ways. One problem I have is that precisely at the point when I most need speech to stand my ground, speech will fail me. This matters when it comes to speaking about autism: as an autistic person who passes, I'm constantly finding that my right to do so is called into question. I'm thinking, for example, about an evening I spent in a town in the Midlands a couple of years ago. I was presenting my work in a library as part of a poetry festival. In the first half of the evening, I read from my new poetry collection, *The Autistic Alice*; in the second half, a local publisher and bookseller interviewed me about my memoir, *Small Pieces*, in which I addressed my brother's suicide and its aftermath.

After dinner with a couple of friends, I presented myself at the library. My interviewer arrived. I left my things in an office and got fitted with a mic. The audience filed in. I was introduced, and stepped up onto the small stage in front of the lectern, poetry book in hand. I did what I always do: I smiled at the audience and made eye contact (they taught us how to do that at my private school, as part of Public Speaking); I said thank you; I said how pleased I was to be there, about my literary connections to the town and how much I valued them. I explained that *The Autistic Alice* was made of three parts, of which two were sequences: 'The Oxygen Man' about my brother's death, and the title sequence, which addressed my experiences as a child growing up with undiagnosed autism. I read several poems from each sequence. The first half finished.

There was a book stall. People went to buy books and, after a quick break, I went to sign them and answer questions. A woman came up to – I mean right up to – me and began firing questions, one after the other, straight into my face. Why did I think I was autistic? What on earth was it about me that made me think I was autistic? I know I replied, but my memory of my own words is not as vivid as that of her anger, so I can't remember what I said. I might have said that I had realized when I saw myself in the autobiographical writings of other autistic women. Experience was not a good-enough answer. She had taught an autistic girl once, and I was nothing like her – this girl had to have a laptop in class, this girl never spoke – I was speaking, therefore I was not like this girl. I may have said that I felt different, because the woman said at some point something like 'but isn't that just being creative?' I must have mentioned my actual diagnosis by a psychologist employed by the NHS, but I seem to remember that that would not do either. I could not possibly be what I said I was, and that seemed to make the woman very angry. I could have suggested she take it up with the NHS; instead I allowed her to put me on the back foot, and keep me there.

The interrogation came to an end when someone came to fetch me – the second half was about to begin. The publisher asked me questions about *Small Pieces*, the story behind it, the process of making it, my family, my Jewishness and how that informed the book. I probably said at some point, because I usually do, that the book did help me to work through my grief to some extent, and part of that was realizing that I would never truly know why my brother took his own life. What I do remember very clearly is that – at some point, before or during the questions – I mentioned that my brother had been diagnosed with ADD (ADHD as it's now known), and that same angry woman said, very audibly, 'Ah, so there was a reason why he killed himself.'

So there you have it: it makes no sense that a diagnosable individual should write books and speak in public; it does, however, make perfect sense that they should meet an early and unnatural death.

Unlike the angry woman, I do not believe that my brother died because of a diagnosis. But I know for certain that you did.

'Diagnosis' is a word coined for professionals – doctors and psychologists and the like – and it has its roots in ancient Greek. Here's what the *Collins English Dictionary* has to say about it:

diagnosis

noun

Word forms: plural -ses (-siːz)

1. a. the identification of diseases by the examination of symptoms and signs and by other investigations

b. an opinion or conclusion so reached

2. a. thorough analysis of facts or problems in order to gain understanding and aid future planning

b. an opinion or conclusion reached through such analysis

3. a detailed description of an organism, esp a plant, for the purpose of classification

gaining understanding: *What is the matter with you?*
future planning: *What are we going to do with you?*

What is the matter with you?
You have been diagnosed with idiocy. You are an idiot.

When you were three, you contracted meningitis, an infection from which, according to your brief online biography, you 'never recovered'. Presumably whatever capacity to speak you might have had was lost. In the twenties, when you were a teenager, you were sent to the Wiesloch sanatorium in your home province of Baden-Württemberg.

In 1934, there was a change of management at Wiesloch, and Dr Wilhelm Mockel, a member of the Nazi Party, took over as medical director. One of his main tasks was to oversee the implementation of the new Law for the Prevention of Hereditary Diseases, and he was sufficiently zealous in this commission that over the next ten years, 1,359 patients at Wiesloch were sterilized.[56] There is no indication that you were among this number, perhaps because your condition had an identifiable origin in a non-hereditary illness. I am also assuming that the detailed family chart the staff made showed no trace of any signs of degeneracy (Jewishness aside). After all, your father Moritz was described as a leader of the Jewish community in your hometown of Konstanz, while your half-brother Erich was a distinguished writer, who would one day return to Konstanz from Israel to found a Jewish library.

In 1938, another doctor, Gregor Overhamm, moved to Wiesloch from Emmendingen. He examined you that year, and his notes survive. Overhamm recorded your diagnosis of 'idiocy', describing you in his own words as 'terribly difficult and disruptive'. He concluded with the following judgement, emphasized with an exclamation mark: '*Lebensunwertes Leben!*'

'Life unworthy of life!'

Your story pivots around these two concepts: 'idiocy' and '*Lebensunwertes Leben*'. Around these two concepts, and the assumed connection between them.

These days, the word 'idiot' is an insult, pure and simple, but there was a time when 'idiot' and 'idiocy' were respectable words, official terms. Like 'diagnosis', it's a Greek word:

C13: from Latin *idiōta* ignorant person, from Greek *idiōtēs* private person, one who lacks professional knowledge, ignoramus; see idio-[57]

I've been reading Patrick McDonagh's history of this concept – of idiocy, of idiots – that we still throw around so casually when we want to insult someone or discredit their opinions.[58] It's a story full of twists and turns, contradictions and fluctuations – it changes, as all concepts do, with the historical context. What is clear is that 'idiocy' was a legal term long before it became a diagnosis, and it is this legal context which accounts for its derivation from the Greek for 'private person'. In the fourteenth century, when the Court of Chancery declared someone an 'idiot', it was a declaration that such a person was unable to perform certain tasks that might be expected of an adult capable of holding property, such as handling money or 'identifying lineage'. They were therefore unfit to take any part in public life, to be a 'public person'. An idiot in fourteenth-century England was a full-grown person who was not considered competent to handle his own affairs – I say 'his', because at the time, as McDonagh points out, a woman was assumed to be incompetent in this sense, regardless of how well she could count.

That is not to say that she could not also be declared an idiot. If she had property or money or both, then such a declaration might still be necessary. Adelheid, meet another weird sister of ours – Emma de Beston, a Cambridgeshire woman examined for idiocy in July 1383:

The said Emma, being caused to appear before them, was asked whence she came and said that she did not know. Being asked in what town she was, she said that she was at Ely. Being asked how many days there were in the week, she said seven but could not name them. Being asked how many husbands she had had in her time she said three, giving the name of one only and not knowing the names of the others. Being asked whether she had ever had issue by them, she said that she had a husband with a son, but did not know his name. Being asked how many shillings there were in forty pence, she said she did not know. Being asked whether she would rather have twenty silver groats than forty pence, she said they were of the same value. They examined her in all other ways which they thought best and found that she was not of sound mind, having neither sense nor memory nor sufficient intelligence to manage herself, her lands or her goods. As appeared by inspection she had the face and countenance of an idiot.[59]

Poor Emma. Her examination must have been a bewildering, even terrifying experience. The process would have been set in motion by a local official or royal commissioner, perhaps after a petition by Emma's family. He would have directed the Sheriff of the County of Cambridgeshire to appoint a day and summon a jury of at least twelve respectable men to meet at a 'convenient and open place'. The officials would have asked the questions and the jury would have made the judgement. If I were hauled out in public to be asked personal questions in front of a dozen strange men, I might not perform so well either. Perhaps my speech would falter. Perhaps I would look funny – ha-ha or peculiar or both. Perhaps they would think I too had 'the face and countenance of an idiot'.

The respectable men of the jury clearly believed that a relative lack of mental capacity was something that could be read in the face and its expression. Emma was declared an idiot not just because her answers suggested that she lacked the understanding necessary to manage her own affairs, but also because she looked different in some way. As these were members of the community and not specialists, this difference would have been assumed to be perceptible to ordinary, 'respectable' persons. What we would now call 'common sense'. Professional expertise was not required to make someone an idiot. It was not then a term of anyone's art.

A century-and-a-half after Emma's examination, an English legal dictionary defined 'idiot' as follows:

> Idiot is he that is a foole naturally from his birth and knoweth not how to accompt of number 20 pence nor cannot name hys father, or mother, nor of what age hymselfe is, or such like easie and common matters; soe that it appereth he has no manner of understanding of reason, nor governement of himselfe, what is for his profit or disprofit.[60]

Unable to name relatives or count change; unable to look after himself; lacking knowledge of 'easy and common' matters expected of an adult – the essential criteria for idiocy had not changed since Emma was examined. But the social context in which the judgement is made was to become broader. In Emma's time, there was no need to attribute the legal status of idiocy to anyone who had neither property nor money – who had no 'affairs' to manage. However, with the introduction of the first Poor Laws under Elizabeth I, it became necessary to distinguish those who could work from those who supposedly would not, so as to separate those paupers who were entitled to receive subsistence directly from the parish from those who must be sent to the workhouse to earn it. Disability in England, whether physical, mental or intellectual, was gradually becoming a public matter, a state concern and an area of moral suspicion. The problem which an 'idiot' presented, at this point, was framed not in medical or scientific terms, but in economic ones.

What is the matter with you?
You cannot support yourself; you are a non-productive burden.

The Nazis didn't beat about the bush: they called you and people like you 'useless eaters'. In her book *Asperger's Children: The Origins of Autism in Nazi Vienna*, Edith Sheffer cites the following question from a maths textbook, issued to schools in Germany and Austria in the thirties: 'An idiot in an institution costs around four Reichsmarks a day. How much would it cost if he has to be cared for there for forty years?'[61]

It might make me and my contemporaries feel better to think of Nazis and Nazi logic as monstrous, an aberration, but they were only building on arguments that had already been made, and not only in Germany. The Industrial Revolution began in Britain, after all, and with it the demand that human beings take on the uniform, productive efficiency of the machines they worked on.

Neither have we stopped making those arguments. Journalist Frances Ryan has written about the effects of contemporary British governments' 'austerity' policies, which operate on the assumption that the deficits in the public purse are best addressed, not by raising taxes, facilitating production or stimulating demand, but by cutting back public spending. In her book *Crippled*, she writes:

disabled people are caught between two entirely contradictory stereotypes. On the one hand, we are pitiable and infirm,
incapable of holding positions of influence or of making a
capitalist contribution. On the other, we are lazy and wilful
scroungers, leaching off the hard-working non-disabled
public. This heightened noticeably as austerity measures
began to roll out with a particular focus on out-of-work sickness and unemployment benefits. It was as if disabled people
were simultaneously pitied for their infirmity and vilified as
a useless burden; judged as incapable of basic tasks by non-
disabled people and criticized for not being in employment.[62]

It's a harrowing book. Some people starve to death as a result
of these policies. Others find themselves under pressure to move
from their own homes to institutions, where all the offensively
unproductive people can be cheaply warehoused, out of the way
and out of sight.

What shall we do with you?
Make you disappear.

In their essay 'Losing', autistic advocate Mel Baggs describes the
first hours of their first stay at a mental institution, as they waited
alone in a bare room while their paperwork was completed by staff:

> Throughout the wait, I become aware I still exist. I haven't
> disappeared. I agreed to admission because I thought dis-
> appearing might be easier than suicide. It didn't work. I'm
> still here.
>   Crazy people are supposed to disappear. People disappear
> when they go in the front door of an institution. But I'm

still here. I don't understand. I'm afraid. I often get things wrong. I know in my bones I'll never be normal. I must be crazy. But crazy people in institutions vanish off the face of the earth. Everything in my whole life has told me this.[63]

I can understand why Baggs was so shocked by their continued existence. People do disappear into institutions – they are 'put away' or 'binned'. Out of sight, out of the way, out of common humanity. Institutionalization can be a form of social death and death was what Baggs wished for. What they are coming to realize in this passage is that just because society no longer feels for you, it doesn't automatically mean that you no longer feel for yourself – nothing as merciful as that.

Mel Baggs goes on to quote another well-known autistic advocate, Cal Montgomery. Baggs and Montgomery have experienced life from both sides: as passing, speaking autistics but also as non-speaking, non-passing autistics (these things can fluctuate, across a lifetime, a year, a day or even an hour). Cal Montgomery has experienced institutions from both sides – as a worker, and as a resident – and has come to the conclusion that they should not exist. As he explains it, even the kindest, most qualified, most talented, most well-meaning staff will struggle to connect with individuals when they have large numbers in their care. When you lack the necessary time and attention to get to know someone with high support needs, someone who doesn't communicate in the usual way, it becomes too easy to write them off. (I don't suppose that Dr Overhamm spent much time with you before he declared you an idiot, and your life unworthy.)

If it were just a matter of insufficient time and attention, it would be bad enough, but the reality is that not all staff are kind, qualified, talented or well meaning. When social care is as poorly paid and poorly resourced as it is in the UK (and no doubt elsewhere), and has such low status and such poor working conditions, staff turnover is often high and staffing numbers low. Social care employers – usually private companies with public contracts – have to take what they can get. And the residents have to suffer for it.

Every few years, there's another scandal, another exposé, when the residents of one institution or another come briefly into sight and into mind, and an institution is closed, and individual staff are disciplined or even prosecuted, and there is an inquiry, and lessons are learned, and new policies are drawn up and something has been seen to be done, but nothing changes. In 2011, it was Winterbourne View. In 2019, it was Whorlton Hall, in County Durham. I watched the BBC's *Panorama* and saw residents with – in the BBC's words – 'autism and learning disabilities' being taunted and provoked by staff, who would then restrain them.[64] I saw a member of staff sit on a young man's chest, take away his glasses and put them on his own face, much to the amusement of his co-workers. I saw a young woman who was afraid of men (I'm sure with very good reason) tormented with the threat of a fictional 'man button', which the staff member could press to summon men to her room. The staff found her distress hilarious, as they also did when they threatened to bring in balloons and burst them – another thing she was afraid of. That cut me inside, because they could have taunted me in exactly the same way – I'm afraid of the sound of bursting balloons. And there was something else distressingly familiar to me: that sick feeling, of being humiliated, of being tormented for someone else's entertainment. Every autistic person will have experienced it at some point. That's what you get when you don't fit. Especially when you are out of sight, out of the way and in someone else's power.

Then people like that can do what they like – the system facilitates it.

And then Covid-19 came along, to make institutions – and disability – hazardous to life and well-being in yet another way. All through spring and early summer in 2020, as we shut schools, workplaces and shops and anywhere else where people might meet in order to slow the spread of the disease, it was spreading fastest in care homes, and for a long time this passed almost without notice; care workers could not access adequate protection for themselves or for the people they supported. The same Act that closed the workplaces suspended local authorities' legal requirement to provide disabled people in the community with appropriate care; even those who were able to access care could hardly follow the advice to socially distance from the people who were helping with their intimate needs. News broadcasts, articles and official statements on the progress of the pandemic stressed that most who died were 'elderly or had underlying conditions' so as to reassure everyone else that most of the people who were dying were just the sort of people who were destined to die in any case.

In November 2020, a report from Public Health England revealed the appalling fact that people with learning disabilities were dying of coronavirus at more than six times the rate of the general population. Earlier that year, the Care Quality Commission had noted that the average age of death for those with autism and learning disabilities was also considerably lower than it was for the population as a whole. But that's nothing new, unfortunately: in 2016, a study in Sweden showed the average age of death for a person with autism spectrum disorder (ASD) to be fifty-four years, compared with seventy for matched controls. The leading causes of death for those considered to be 'low-functioning' were neurological conditions such as epilepsy; for 'high-functioning' fortunates like me, it was suicide. These are not the sort of premature deaths that are either unavoidable or unforeseeable. It's possible to save these lives – all we need to do is get everyone to agree that it's worth the effort.

What is wrong with you?
You are 'more like an animal than a person'. You do not meet the criteria for personhood.

My mother told me, more than once, that any decision a Jew makes should be informed by the concept of *pikuach nefesh*, by the principle that the duty to preserve human life trumps all others: it meant that you could eat forbidden food if the alternative was starving, that an ill person didn't have to fast on Yom Kippur, and that – in general – you could break a law, religious or secular, if the purpose of doing so was to save a life. The Talmud tells us that 'whoever kills one life kills the world entire, and whoever saves one life saves the world entire'.

My mother also taught me about Kashrut, the kosher or dietary laws. They determine, among other things, which animals we are allowed to eat, and the correct way to slaughter them. Jews are not supposed to hunt for sport, as we are not supposed to take pleasure in killing animals, but we are allowed to kill them. One of the clear distinctions between a person and an animal is that animal life is not sacred.

So if you want a reasonable measure of safety, you'd better make sure people notice you're human. This holds whether you're Jewish or not. The precise nature of that distinction, between animal and person, is a bone that philosophers have gnawed on again and again. When I was an undergraduate, I remember learning something along the following lines:

Aristotle said that humans were an animal (zoon), but a particularly complex and sophisticated animal, being both a political animal (politikon zoon) and a thinking, or reasoning animal (logikon zoon). This makes for difference significant enough to be categorical: humans reason, and organize ourselves into rule-bound polities.

The human/beast distinction based on the capacity to reason comes up again and again, generally with the understanding – stated or assumed – that the capacity to reason places us in an elevated position relative to other animals in the way that other capacities – to fly, or see in the dark, leap three times our height, or communicate by changing our skin colour – would not. The human/beast distinction is not only categorical but hierarchical. As it says in Genesis 1:26:

> And God said, Let us make man in our image, after our likeness: and let them have dominion over the fish of the sea, and over the fowl of the air, and over the cattle, and over all the earth, and over every creeping thing that creepeth upon the earth.[65]

Human beings are nearer to God than animals are. There's a divine order, in Christian terms the Great Chain of Being, which sounds horizontal, but being hierarchical, is perhaps more clearly expressed vertically:

God
Angels
Demons (being angels, but fallen)
Stars
The Moon

Kings
Princes
Nobles
Commoners
Wild Animals
Domesticated Animals
Trees
Other Plants
Precious Stones
Precious Metals
Other Minerals

And once you've established this most basic structural principle, of things being ordered vertically, hierarchically, it will only seem proper and natural, whatever the scale or context.

If this order is divine, then God is its justification. If you put God to one side, you need to work a bit harder to justify it. When John Locke wrote his 'Essay Concerning Human Understanding' in the 1670s, he conceptualized the difference between human and beast in terms that recall Aristotle: human beings are reasonable beings. While animals and human beings share the capacity to receive and respond to sensory information, it is only human beings who have the higher-order capacities that enable us to take that information and think with it.

As he formulated a model of the process by which sense impressions became thoughts, Locke set out another hierarchy – the historian C. F. Goodey calls it 'a hierarchical chain of abstract psychological perfection',[66] and it looks like this:

abstraction
enlarging

composition
comparing
discerning
retention
perception

According to Locke, this is how specific pieces of sensory information become knowledge which can be generally applied: starting at the bottom of the ladder, with perception, the sense impression is subject to a series of increasingly complex and sophisticated mental operations, until it becomes an abstraction. When you place this hierarchy next to the Great Chain of Being, you can see how it functions as a rationale for the relative positions of human being/man and animal/beast/brute:

man   abstraction
enlarging
composition
comparing
discerning
retention
brutes perception

So Locke says: 'This I think I may be positive in, That the power of Abstracting is not at all in [Brutes]; and that the having of general Ideas, is that which puts a perfect distinction betwixt Man and Brutes; and is an Excellency which the Faculties of Brutes do by no means attain to'.[67] As an empiricist, he needs to show the evidence behind this assertion about the limited capacities of beasts, and he points to their having 'no use of Words, or any other general Signs'.

As Goodey points out, Locke 'never quite says "Idiots abstract not"',[68] but it is obvious that anyone who locates the 'perfect distinction' between human beings and (other) animals in the possession of general ideas, evidenced by the 'use of Words, or any other general Signs', has placed any human individual who lacks speech in a somewhat precarious position. I find this particular passage, which Goodey quotes, quite chilling:

> To say, that a rational Animal is capable of Conversation, is all one, as to say, a Man. But no one will say, That Rationality is capable of Conversation, because it makes not the whole Essence, to which we give the name Man.
> There are Creatures in the World, that have shapes like ours, but are hairy, and want Language, and Reason. There are Naturals amongst us, that have perfectly our shape, but want Reason, and some of them language too.[69]

Naturals (i.e. idiots) are among us, and have 'our shape' but they are not us. The first person plural is a protected space, and you have been barred from it.

Believe me, I can understand the glamour of the perfect distinction; I was in thrall to it for far too long. When I picture Carolus Linnaeus, who set up the system for the naming, classifying and ordering of living things some ninety years or so after Locke wrote his Treatises, I imagine him having an absolute whale (order: Cetacea) of a time. There is such joy to be had in sorting, in differentiating like from nearly like, in the placing of objects in relation to each other, in the making of a coherent arrangement. It begins as a functional pleasure, the feeling of performing an effective action, and culminates in aesthetic pleasure, of apprehending a whole in which all the parts chime harmoniously with each other. Some people worry when autistic children line things up, and worry that what they are seeing is evidence of anxiety, or rigidity of thought, or lack of imagination. They see it as a pathological behaviour, when actually they are witnessing joy – the kind of joy that motivated Linnaeus. And when that child tells you about the arrangement, they are seeking to share that joy.

You don't always have to arrange things yourself to experience it. Just seeing things pre-arranged in a harmonious order is enough to get at least a small hit. When I was at primary school, we were taught to read through a series of books called *Through the Rainbow*, and while I couldn't tell you anything about the content, I'm still nostalgic for the covers. In Reception class, they gave us coloured wooden Cuisenaire rods to teach us to count, and I miss them too. Sometimes I go to John Lewis just to enjoy the spectral arrangement of towels.

Why do people assume that order is antithetical to play? Is it because of its association with systems compulsorily learned: the alphabet, the numbers on the clock, phonics, times tables, the periodic table, historical dates, Linnaean classifications…? When it is intelligence that is being assessed, rather than the capacity for acceptable play, then the ability to order, to differentiate between objects and arrange them accordingly, is seen as a good thing. I've been praised for this myself, and I've enjoyed the praise, even as an adult. In my early twenties, when I found myself adrift – not for the first time – I went to see an occupational psychologist. (All those childhood visits to consulting rooms – of which more later – had established in me a belief that consulting rooms were the places where self-knowledge was reliably found, and submitting to professional expertise was the way to find it.) She set me an aptitude test: sorting a bag of counters. She emptied the bag onto the floor, and told me to arrange its contents in any way I saw fit.

I examined the counters, and saw that they had stickers on them in a range of colours; when I looked closer, I saw that each sticker had one of a range of symbols on it. So I knew what to do then: I sorted them into colour groups first, and then I arranged the counters together so that the colours were on one axis, and the symbols on another. As there were more of some colours than others, and more with certain symbols than others, they made a pleasing, regular diamond shape. I was happy with the shape and happy with myself for having made it. The occupational psychologist told me that most people sorted according to either colour or shape and that the way I had arranged the counters was therefore 'special'. Not weird – special. I left that consulting room with a sense that I had great potential but, sad to say, I have never found a job which consisted of arranging counters.

Say there had been another counter in the bag, one with a sticker of an indeterminate colour, or carrying a symbol that didn't seem to bear any relation to the others, or resembled more than one of the others equally; when I failed to find a place in my otherwise harmonious system for this counter, where would I have located that failure – in the system, in me, or in the counter? Would I have resented the way the counter made my lovely system look suddenly incomplete? Would I have had an urge to throw the counter away?

What are we going to do with you?
Conduct an experiment.

Emma was examined by a jury of respectable men; you were examined by doctors. Reading Locke – who was a physician as well as a political philosopher – has given me some sense of how this transition, from legal status to diagnosis, was set in train. Goodey points out that, in the process, the sense of the scope of an idiot's incompetence expanded in such a way as to engulf the individuals to whom it was ascribed, and place them outside the realm of human nature. As he puts it:

> Whereas the idiot of feudal or Tudor fiscal notions was someone incapable of being initiated in a particular skill, incapable of understanding something specific, Locke's is incapable of understanding, full stop. This is… an absolute rejection of psychology's being applicable in this case (whereas madness illuminates the operations and associations of ideas magnificently)… To the extent that amentia lies beyond what is human, psychology is now no more relevant to the individuals who embody it than to cockles and oysters.[70]

For a long time, it was assumed that nothing could be done to improve the condition of individuals who were judged to have 'amentia' – to be literally 'mindless'. They remained of little interest to medical science, and the words 'idiot', 'imbecile' and 'natural fool' were applied interchangeably. Precision in differential diagnosis only becomes necessary where there are decisions to be made about treatment or management, and there was very little of either.

Then, one day in 1797, three woodsmen working in the forest near Saint-Sernin-sur-Rance in Southern France captured a speechless boy who had been living wild among the trees. Over the next few years, various people would try their best to care for him, but he could not settle, and escaped back to the woods on eight separate occasions. He was taken to Paris, where he became an object of great scientific, philosophical and general curiosity. Eventually he was taken up by the physician Jean-Marc Gaspard Itard. Itard had worked with Abbé Sicard at his Institute for Deaf Mutes, where he had observed at first hand that a group long believed to be beyond help could, with the right techniques, be trained and educated to a high level. He hypothesized that if he applied an adapted version of Sicard's system, he would succeed in moving the wild boy, now named 'Victor', from his apparent near-animal condition to that of a civilized and reasonable human being, equipped with the language necessary to formulate and communicate ideas. He hoped that, in doing so, he might shed new light on the nature of the distinction between human and animal which had so exercised Locke and continued to perplex the natural philosophers who followed him. And so an experiment in remedial education began.

Itard devised a programme of activities for Victor, intended to foster a taste for social life with his fellow human beings, develop his senses, accustom him to receiving direction and so, it was hoped, 'lead him to the use of speech'.[71] While Itard took charge of Victor's formal training, he shared responsibility for the boy's overall care with his *gouvernante* (nursemaid), Mme Guerin. They had very different relationships with their charge. Itard sought to impress his authority upon the boy, using his approval and disapproval as teaching tools, to make it clear when a rule of civilized or rational conduct had been transgressed. Mme Guerin, on the other hand, occupied a more conventional motherly role. As the development of Victor's appetite for society and his capacity for human affection was such an important part of Itard's project, this role was vital. McDonagh quotes a passage from the first of Itard's two reports on Victor's education, in which he writes of the importance of kindness in the pursuit of their aims. He praises Mme Guerin as one who cared for Victor 'with the patience of a mother, and the intelligence of an enlightened instructor'. Although this was not enough to prevent Victor's running away for two weeks, his response to her when he returned shows how much she must have meant to him:

> Victor had barely seen his gouvernante before he turned pale and briefly lost consciousness; but sensing her embrace... he suddenly revived and expressed his joy by shrill cries, convulsive grasping of his hands and a beaming, radiant face. He presented this image, to the eyes of all around, less of a fugitive returned by force to the supervision of his guardian than a loving son who, of his own desire, was throwing himself into the arms of she who had given him life.[72]

This touching scene comes from Itard's second report. Reading it, you get a picture of Victor as a rounded human character, full of complex and sometimes contradictory emotions, so it saddened me to read that Itard judged his experiment to be a failure and Victor to be the uneducable 'refuse of nature'. Victor had learned a great deal: his sensory capacities had improved; he was able to use sounds, signs and gestures to express his needs and convey affection, gratitude and, when required, remorse; he was able to take instruction. But he was never able to speak more than a very few, isolated words, and after a few frustrating years, Itard called off his experiment. Victor was left to live out the rest of his days (happily, I hope) with Mme Guerin.

Itard's ultimate aim had been to take Victor and render him indistinguishable from his fellow human beings, in the way that he behaved, and the way that he communicated. He had not succeeded in doing so, but, as he acknowledged himself, he and Mme Guerin had seen significant changes in Victor's sensory capacities, his expressive ability and his behaviour. Although Itard did not himself believe that idiots were educable, as his reports were disseminated, his meticulous records of Victor's work and progress fed into a growing feeling that such children could, and should, be trained. In 1840, Itard's pupil Edouard Séguin set up a school for children with intellectual disabilities, and in 1846 he published *Traitement moral, hygiène, et éducation des idiots et des autres enfants arriérés*. This was the first textbook of its kind, and was soon translated into English as *The Moral Treatment, Hygiene, and Education of Idiots and Other Backward Children*. The wording makes me wince, but for its time, the book represented a significant step forward. Séguin's methods helped many pupils to develop what we would now call the 'life skills' or 'self-care skills' they needed in order to leave institutions and live successfully with their families.

Across Europe, further institutions were founded along similar lines. Between the late 1840s and the late 1860s, five large, voluntary institutions, known as 'idiot asylums', appeared across England. You could see these as part of a greater human project under way in Victorian Britain, whereby problematic individuals, whether mad or criminal or feeble in mind, could be sorted into their various categories and placed accordingly in their respective institutions where the right prescription of good air, good nutrition, hard work and moral instruction would transform them into fitter members of society. In a country where everything was running ever faster and more efficiently, where railways had necessitated that everyone keep to the same time and the telegraph had made this possible, where machines increasingly set the pace and rhythm of human labour, what was needed was a population that was healthy, trainable and steady enough in its habits to keep Britain's empire and economy going and growing.

Which brings us circling back to something I mentioned earlier: the demand that human beings take on the uniform, productive efficiency of the machines they worked on. On that count, I'm afraid we both fail.

What is the matter with you?
You do not conform to the standard – you are not normal.

Standard mass production requires a mass of standard productive people – fleshy components that fit the machine. And if any one component, whether it's made of iron or steel or flesh, should slip out of place or stall, the whole thing grinds to halt. So you need to keep measuring things to make sure that they fit and are working at the correct speed. You need an agreed set of standards against which to measure things, so that you can tell when they deviate from it. If they do, you have identified a problem that you need to fix.

Like the telegraph and the steamship, normality is a Victorian invention. I learned this from reading Lennard J. Davis, disability scholar and normality (or 'normalcy') expert. Here he is on the history of the term:

> I begin with the rather remarkable fact that the constellation of words describing this concept 'normal,' 'normalcy,' 'normality,' 'norm,' 'average,' 'abnormal' – all entered the European languages rather late in human history. The word 'normal' as 'constituting, conforming to, not deviating or different from, the common type or standard, regular, usual' only enters the English language around

1840. (Previously, the word had meant 'perpendicular'; the carpenter's square, called a 'norm,' provided the root meaning.) Likewise, the word 'norm,' in the modern sense, has only been in use since around 1855, and 'normality' and 'normalcy' appeared in 1849 and 1857, respectively. If the lexicographical information is relevant, it is possible to date the coming into consciousness in English of an idea of 'the norm' over the period 1840–1860.[73]

So, in the same period that the Victorians were standardizing time and building idiot asylums, they were calling the norm into being. And you cannot do that without summoning its shadow, the abnormal.

In the 1860s and '70s, the Victorians trained their talent for productivity and standardization onto the school system. In 1880, education became compulsory for all children aged between five and ten. This made many things possible for the first time: mass literacy was one; the establishment of a benchmark for normal cognitive development was another. Not only possible, but necessary. For efficiency in mass production, you need your employees to work at more or less the same speed. For efficiency in mass education, you need your pupils to learn and develop at more or less the same rate. Hence the emergence of a new problem in need of a solution: the slow or 'backward' child.

There were degrees of backwardness, of course, degrees of deviance from the norm. The optimism regarding the educability of idiots which had inspired the establishment of the mid-century asylums had begun to fade somewhat, as it had become clear that some of the inmates, like Victor, would never be able to speak, or read, or learn a trade (boys) or be prepared for domestic service (girls). The vocabulary around cognitive impairment needed to be refined in order to distinguish the normally educable from the partly educable, the partly educable from the ineducable, the potential self-supporters and producers from those whose survival must always depend on the generosity of their families, or charity, or the state.

The identification of differing levels of cognitive impairment had begun earlier in the century, in the work of another French father of psychiatry, Jean-Etienne Dominique Esquirol. In his textbook on insanity, published in 1838, Esquirol described two levels of impairment: idiocy and imbecility. 'Imbeciles' were 'generally well formed, and their organization is nearly normal. They enjoy the use of the intellectual and affective faculties, but in less degree than the perfect man, and they can be developed only to a certain extent.' Idiots, on the other hand, were 'incapable of attention' and 'cannot control their senses. They hear, but do not understand; they see, but do not regard. Having no ideas, and thinking not, they have nothing to desire; therefore have no need of signs, nor of speech.'[74]

Note how the lack of speech is taken as evidence of a lack of language and a lack of thoughts worth having. I've mentioned that speech fails me sometimes. That's why I prefer to write.

By 1909, when an Abstract of the Report of the Royal Commission on the Care and Control of the Feeble-Minded was published, the broader term 'mental defective' had come into use, but there were sub-divisions within this category, as suggested by the Royal College of Physicians. Some of these, taken together, make up yet another hierarchy, another ladder:

(3) 'Idiots,' i.e., persons so deeply defective in mind from birth or from an early age that they are unable to guard

themselves from common physical dangers, such as, in the case of young children, would prevent their parents from leaving them alone.

(4) 'Imbeciles,' i.e., persons who are capable of guarding themselves against common physical dangers, but who are incapable of earning their own living by reason of mental defect existing from birth or from an early age.

(5) 'Feeble-minded,' i.e., persons who may be capable of earning a living under favourable circumstances, but are incapable from mental defect existing from birth or from an early age: (a) of competing on equal terms with their normal fellows; or (b) of managing themselves and their affairs with ordinary prudence.[75]

There are echoes of earlier definitions of idiot here, in the emphasis on the capacity to earn and the reference to a lack of 'ordinary prudence' reminiscent of the case of Emma de Beston, but the inability to compete 'on equal terms with their normal fellows' is a newer criterion, associated with the arrival of compulsory education and with it, the 'backward child'.

By the time I, a weird and precocious child, came across the differential definitions of 'imbecile' and 'idiot' in our household copy of *Pears' Cyclopaedia* somewhen in the eighties, they had acquired relative numerical values. They had IQ ranges next to them.

What is the matter with you?
You are a statistical outlier.

*

When I was nine, I was assigned my own numerical value and it seemed like the answer to all my weird child problems.

Although I had been discharged by the speech therapist, I was still unhappy at school. We had to go in to lunch in twos, and nobody would go in with me, which meant I kept being sent to the back of the queue. I found a solution to this problem by agreeing to accompany another girl in my class, who was physically disabled (a rare thing in mainstream schools at the time) and so was allowed in with or without a partner. Being her partner was seen by the other girls as a good deed, something she should be grateful for. I was grateful to her. I saw no reason to condescend. We had a shared stigma as misfit clever girls and that drew us together. We were allowed to spend our lunchtimes playing chess in the corridor outside the headmaster's office, and when she was well and at school, I could cope with being there. When she was ill and away, being there was a torment. I would convince myself every morning that I had a stomach ache or a headache, that I could not possibly go in.

Later on, I learned that it was my new friend's mother, herself a teacher, who suggested that my parents take me to see an educational psychologist. They took me to a private practice in Great James Street. I remember being impressed by the street, and by the building. I remember sitting by myself, working through a book of puzzles, and enjoying it very much. I remember that after I'd finished, the psychologist, a white-haired serious man, looked over my work, and told me I might have made even fewer mistakes if I had not been in such a hurry. I remember registering that I had been told off about the way I approached my work, something I was used to. I remember going into a room with a young woman to try and replicate pictures with a set of blocks and being mesmerized by the sight of her long, red shiny nails as she reached over to scramble the blocks ready for another picture. Despite the mild telling off, which anyway had been mitigated by the news that I'd done well, it was a good day. Interesting tasks, unobtrusively attentive adults and no other kids – just the way I liked it.

The ed psych must have thought it was a good day too, because he assigned me a high numerical value, both in terms of IQ points and in terms of my learning 'ages': when I was reading, I was 14.0 years old, when I was spelling I was 11.5, and when I was doing mental arithmetic I was 13.0.

Not that any of that helped me the rest of the time.

What is the matter with you?
Your development is out of sync.

The concept of mental age pre-dates the IQ scale. It appeared in the early years of the twentieth century and came out of the work of Alfred Binet, director of the psychology department at the Sorbonne. Mass education provided him with both a large sample to measure and a purpose for the measurement: to identify those children who would be liable to fall significantly behind relative to their peers, and would therefore need separate, specialist educational provision or extra help. In 1904, the French government commissioned him to undertake a preliminary study, with a view to developing a set of techniques for identifying struggling children. For Binet, the emphasis was not on identifying deficits, but assessing needs. (There is nothing wrong in assessing needs; neither is there anything wrong with having them.)

Binet and his team assembled a series of short tasks. He avoided any which might assess purely learned skills, such as reading.

Instead, to use Stephen Jay Gould's words, test subjects were faced with a 'hodgepodge of diverse activities', in the hope that a wide enough mixture of tests would enable Binet to 'abstract a child's general potential with a single score'.[76] The hodgepodge included tests which might have been recognizable to the men who examined Emma de Beston, as they assessed ordinary everyday skills such as counting money. They also included tests in which the cultural bias would be obvious to anyone who came across them now, such as the one that involved judging which of two female faces was the more attractive. Along with the other tests, it was deployed as part of a series of thirty questions, placed in order of ascending difficulty, and administered only by properly trained examiners. By the time the second edition appeared in 1908, Binet had assigned an age level to each task, supposed to correspond to the youngest age at which a child of 'normal intelligence' should be able to complete it. The last task a given child was able to complete was thus indicative of that child's 'mental', as opposed to chronological, age.

All Binet was trying to do was to identify schoolchildren who were falling behind their peers academically at a particular point in their education, but over time, the notion of a 'mental age' broadened, until it came to represent a judgement of the permanent and unchanging degree of an adult's capacity to be an adult.

What is the matter with you?
Despite your adult body, you will never be an adult.

In their introduction to a recent collection of essays written by, for and about women with intellectual disabilities, the editors write that '[s]ometimes the needs and wants of women with intellectual disabilities are not known by those around them because other people do not see them as *women*'.[77] They go on to draw attention to a shameful truth, which is that, by and large, both feminism and disability studies have failed to take account of the lives and the experiences of women like you.

The failure to see you as a woman goes hand in hand with the failure to see you as an adult. I say failure, but often it's better described as a refusal. Jen Slater, Embla Ágústsdóttir and Freyja Haraldsdóttir see this refusal as arising from 'the dangerous ableist heteronormativity of adulthood and womanhood driven by binary gendered, ableist, racialized and classed constructs of independence, financial self-sufficiency, property ownership and normative family relations, including parenthood'. They suggest that 'adulthood itself is not an innate way of being, neither is it wholly age based. Rather, adulthood is an ableist concept, which intersects with identity, embodiment and social positioning'.[78]

What I understand this to mean is that adulthood is not a developmental stage but a social position, and as such cannot be attained or maintained without the support and acknowledgement of others. And what others are acknowledging is not the state of one's innermost psychological, mental or spiritual development – whatever that may mean – but the observable adherence to certain norms, of speech, of behaviour, of appearance, and the successful performance of certain roles. I've often felt ashamed of my failure to meet them – when I look vulnerable in public, for example, or allow myself to be visibly pleased by something that people might normally expect to please a child (the spectral arrangement of towels!). All I risk is humiliation, although that's bad enough. For you, the dangers of ableism and heteronormativity were far more concrete.

We're familiar with the concept of 'mental age' from news reports like this:

A pregnant woman with learning disabilities who was ordered by a judge to abort her baby will now be able to give birth after an appeal.

The woman, who is in her twenties and 22 weeks pregnant, has the mental age of a six- to nine-year-old, a court heard.[79]

I remember this case: it was reported widely, and discussed – with anger and alarm – by many of the disability activists and scholars I follow on Twitter. The woman at the centre of the case was an adult pregnant with a healthy foetus, which she wished to carry to term. There was no indication that the pregnancy was any threat to her physical health. Despite this, a judge ruled that it would be in her best interests to be forced to terminate the pregnancy. They did not believe that the woman was truly capable of understanding what it meant to have and care for a baby, and felt that the trauma of giving birth would be worse for her than the trauma of termination. It was also feared that she might neglect or harm the baby. The woman's mother said that she could care for the baby herself, but the judge did not think that it would be possible for the same person to care for a child and a daughter with 'moderately severe' learning disabilities. Both the woman's mother and her social worker felt that the judge underestimated her capacities. The ruling was overturned, but on the grounds that the grandmother, not the mother, was judged to be capable of caring for the child.

When the educational psychologist who tested me used the concept of 'mental age', he was using it in a very specific way, to assess my performance in specific academic-related areas relative to that of other children of a similar age. When I was nine I was more than averagely good at spelling, reading and mental arithmetic. That was all. If a concept designed to express a measurement of the scholastic capacities of a nine-year-old is used to indicate an adult woman's unfitness for motherhood, then it seems reasonable to question whether or not that concept might be – sometimes – misapplied.

There are adults with learning disabilities who have been asking this question. Here's what Ivanova Smith, who trains medical professionals at the University of Washington, has to say in an article for NOS Magazine:

> For years, medical professionals have told parents of newly diagnosed intellectually disabled people that they would mentally be children for their entire lives. Even though I am a 28-year-old, pregnant, married adult, as well as a faculty member at University of Washington, people still tell me that I think like a child. These words are not just offensive language. They can also take away our rights to normal adult lives. Historically, so-called 'mental age theory' has stripped people with intellectual and developmental disabilities of our dignity, our reproductive freedom and our parental rights. Age theory has also been used to strip us of the rights to make adult choices, such as buying alcohol and tobacco or having sexual relationships.[80]

Regardless of their performance in aptitude tests, an adult is an adult and a child is a child. Regardless of demeanour, too. Ivanova Smith likes to carry plush toys with them as 'comfort items', but they are still an adult. (As are the non-disabled people they encounter who greet the toys with real enthusiasm – who doesn't like a plush toy?) At ten years old, I had a serious air and a penchant for long words, but I was still a child.

Sometimes people forgot this. One day our teacher forgot and left me in charge of the class while she popped out to fetch something from the school office. I can't quite remember how it came about, but by the time she returned a few minutes later, the whole class was in uproar and another girl – I'll call her Sally – had me in a headlock and was calling me her 'little apricot'. Sally was at the opposite end of the class to me academically, but she was a much better entertainer.

Sally was also far better at getting on with the other girls. I think that sometimes they may have laughed at her rather than with her, and I couldn't tell you how she felt about that, but she liked the same music and clothes and games as they did, and was accepted as one of them, which I never was. She was likeable – I liked her, and I couldn't bring myself to be angry with her about the headlock business; I realized that, in contrast to some of the other girls, she didn't dislike me either.

Sally sat in front of the teacher's desk, and I sat at the desk behind. We were headaches, both of us. Neither of us was developing at the normal, convenient speed. We made the system glitch.

—and now I'm glitching, jumping ahead of myself. The Sally debacle happened in my second year of junior school, but the educational psychologist visit took place during the first. In his letter, he predicted the educational system glitch, but discussed it in terms of my capacities rather than the system's. The problem was that 'children such as Joanne... tend to become bored with the content and pace of a normal school curriculum'. The solution was to make sure I was 'adequately stimulated and stretched'.

My mother took the letter to my headmaster, who told her that I was 'an average intelligence child with a personality problem'. (I mentioned earlier that things had deteriorated there.) My class teacher, who prided herself on separating out the brighter kids and drawing attention to their difference at every opportunity, called me to the front of the class and shouted at me because my mother had come 'moaning' to the school. The headmaster called me into his office and shouted at me for pretending to be ill in the mornings, and for 'going through my work like a computer' (no, I still don't know what that means). I was set an essay on a topic of my choice, which I had no idea how to do; naturally I made a mess of it.

My best friend was still often ill. Most of the other children still disliked me. I continued at the school and continued being a problem. During the following year – the Year of the Apricot – my chess-playing friend was away a lot. My chief bully and her gang caught me eating my lunch on a bench behind the prefabs and told the teacher that I had been eating in the toilets. She was not our usual teacher, who was relatively kind, but an older, stricter member of staff who stood in when the others were away. She took the opportunity to use me as a teachable moment (Teacher: What do we say: 'When in Rome...'? Class: '...do as the Romans do!'), told the headmaster and made sure I knew that he was furious. My mother wanted to go to the school and complain – I would not let her, as I knew that I would only get blamed and picked on again.

It was obvious by now that the school was not going to accommodate me, and I would always be unhappy there. The psychologist had written that [Joanne] 'will be best suited by a school where there are not only other pupils, but also teachers, with a level of ability similar to her own'. So my parents remortgaged the house, and moved me to an academic private school, which they had never meant to do. Thanks to the high numerical value assigned to me in that one set of tests on that one day when I was nine, I was given access to a world of great educational, social and cultural privilege; at the same time, I was given to understand that living up to the promise of that high numerical value was both a duty and an entitlement.

Reading the letter in the light of my autism diagnosis, I can see the signs which the psychologist detected but lacked the tools to interpret: 'Throughout testing, it was noticed that Joanne frequently said "what" or "pardon", and it is more than likely that she is suffering from some degree of deafness. I understand that she requires frequent syringing of her ears, and clearly some more attention should be given to the status of her hearing.' I still sometimes miss what people say to me. It's a problem with auditory processing, quite common in autistic people, and nothing to do with hearing as such. Sometimes the sound and the sense come to me in two separate, consecutive packets, one a beat behind the other. I have childhood memories of hearing people's speech turning into goobledygook and back into English again, which I used to think represented holes in my childhood vocabulary, and I now understand to be early memories of auditory processing dysfunction. My expressive language skills are naturally much better than my receptive ones. Effort and maturity have helped me to narrow the gap, but when I was nine it was vast.

Another thing that strikes me now, as I look at the letters from the consulting rooms and remember the awkward scenes from school – the lunch queue, the bullying, the encounter with Sally in front of the class – is not the level of my academic intelligence or, for that matter, the degree of my oral dysfluency, but the extent of my fear. I knew it was dangerous to stand out.

What is the matter with you?
Your fertility is a threat.

After Binet died in 1911, his work was taken up and developed by others. In 1912, a German psychologist, William Stern, changed the statistical method by which a child's final score was calculated, dividing the mental by the chronological age rather than subtracting from it; the resulting measurement is what we have come to call the Intelligence Quotient, or IQ.

While Stern changed the way in which results were reached, other psychologists extended the scope of their interpretation. Binet had never attempted to establish or support any theory about the nature of intelligence; he was not developing a method of ranking the intelligence of normal children; however low a child's score, he never intended it to be taken as an indication of innate and/or permanent incapacity. But IQ would be taken up and used for precisely this purpose. Henry Herbert Goddard and Lewis Terman brought Binet's scale to the USA, developed it into the Stanford–Binet scale and put it to work ranking 1.75 million American soldiers during the First World War; they assigned each man they tested what they took to be a permanent and inherent numerical value, and used the results as support for the theory of innate, inherited intelligence. They then went further, suggesting that the results of mass IQ testing could be used to construct not only hierarchies of individuals, but also hierarchies of groups. Over the following decades, IQ testing would be cited as evidence that men were more intelligent than women, white people were more intelligent than black and brown people, middle-class people were more intelligent than working-class people, and white gentiles were more intelligent than Jews. These researchers believed that these differences between groups were not only stable over a lifetime, but over generations too.

This theory of hereditarian intelligence has its roots in nineteenth-century Britain. When Charles Darwin published *The*

Origin of Species in 1859, one of its most enthusiastic readers was his half-cousin Francis Galton. He was particularly fascinated by the chapter 'Variation under Domestication', on animal breeding, and would spend the rest of his working life developing methods of exploring variation in human populations and generating hypotheses about human heredity, based on what he found there.

I've said how much the Victorians loved to measure things, and Galton was a measurer extraordinaire. When London hosted the International Health Exhibition in 1884, Galton set up his Anthropometric Laboratory. For a small fee, visitors could walk through an interactive exhibit, first filling out a form with personal and family history (age, birthplace, marital status, residence and occupation), and then visiting a series of stations at which measurements were made relating to eye colour, hair colour, eyesight, hearing, touch, breathing capacity, the ability to throw a punch, strength of pulling and squeezing with both hands, heights in various positions (sitting, standing, etc.), arm span and weight. Galton went on to develop new statistical methods to analyse the unprecedented amount of human data he had collected. These methods – or refinements of them – are still in use across the social sciences.

I think it's safe to assume that, in common with Linnaeus – and me – Galton was a person who took great pleasure in placing objects in relation to each other, in achieving coherent and convincing arrangements. He would probably have enjoyed IQ tests, and been extremely good at them: Terman himself estimated Galton's childhood IQ at 200 on the Stanford–Binet scale; the average is 100. He even wrote a paper, 'The Intelligence Quotient of Francis Galton in Childhood', using material from Galton family correspondence to support his estimate. Terman noted with approval Galton's 'superior social class' and commented, 'It is well known that, in general, a high correlation obtains between favourable mental traits of all kinds; that, for example, children superior in intelligence also tend to be superior in moral qualities.'[81] For Terman and his contemporaries, IQ correlated with both social class and moral virtue.

While higher IQ was equated with higher moral worth, lower IQ was thought to be associated with higher fertility. Galton identified this as a problem, and coined a word for the study of possible solutions: 'eugenics'. In 1883, he published his book *Inquiries into Human Faculty and Its Development*, in which he explained the term:

> That is, with questions bearing on what is termed in Greek, *eugenes*, namely, good in stock, hereditarily endowed with noble qualities. This, and the allied words, *eugeneia*, etc., are equally applicable to men, brutes, and plants. We greatly want a brief word to express the science of improving stock, which is by no means confined to questions of judicious mating, but which, especially in the case of man, takes cognisance of all influences that tend in however remote a degree to give to the more suitable races of strains of blood a better chance of prevailing speedily over the less suitable than they otherwise would have had. The word *eugenics* would sufficiently express the idea; it is at least a neater word and more generalised one than viriculture which I once ventured to use.[82]

Positive eugenics: enabling the 'more suitable races of strains of blood' to breed.

Negative eugenics: preventing the rest.

What are we going to do with you?
Prevent you from breeding.

Here's another category from the 1909 list:

(6) 'Moral Imbeciles,' i.e., persons who from an early age display some mental defect coupled with strong vicious or criminal propensities on which punishment has little or no deterrent effect.[83]

When the old Victorian asylums were closed in the 1980s, among the people who emerged, briefly, into public visibility were women who had spent their entire adult lives in institutions, on account of a diagnosis of 'moral imbecility' received decades earlier. The term 'moral imbecility', when applied to girls or women, usually referred to sexual behaviour, and was inextricably bound up with white middle-class anxiety that other types of human being might outbreed them. The innate depravity of these women is seen as the source of this social ill, and their confinement as the solution. Only rarely are the men who have sex with – or rape – these 'feeble-minded' women ever blamed for their conduct, and they are never seen as the location of the problem. Nobody suggests that abusive men should be rounded up and segregated to prevent them breeding. That was the solution the report recommended for the feeble-minded, however, and, following the Mental Deficiency Act of 1913, that was what happened. For example, the archives of the Meanwood Park Hospital, a 'mental deficiency colony' in Leeds, include chilling oral histories from former inmates who were picked up by the Executive Officer in his car one day, and never seen in the wider community again.

Other countries adopted still more drastic and permanent solutions. In the year of the British Mental Deficiency Act, American IQ enthusiast Henry Herbert Goddard published *The Kallikak Family*, a book for general readers, which he subtitled *A Study in the Heredity of Feeble-mindedness*. Goddard believed that his research into the history of the family he named 'The Kallikaks' (from the Greek, meaning 'good bad') had provided him with sound proof of the hereditable nature of feeble-mindedness. It is in this book that we find another of our weird sisters.

Opposite the title page of the book is a photograph of the first family member known to Goddard, a resident of the Training School for Feeble-Minded Girls and Boys at which he worked. Captioned 'Deborah Kallikak, As She Appears To-Day at The Training School', it depicts a beautiful young woman in a white dress; her hair is neatly pinned up, with an enormous bow fastened at the back, spread out like a pair of angel's wings. She is sitting with a cat in her lap and holds an open book in her hands. She has the smallest, most demure smile on her face, and looks out dreamily to the left of the camera. She might be any well-brought-up, slightly self-conscious young lady. You might say she looks eminently marriageable; she is certainly attractive. And that, according to Goddard, is precisely what makes her so dangerous.

Goddard wants the reader to understand that 'the idiot is not our greatest problem. He is indeed loathsome; he is somewhat difficult to take care of; nevertheless, he lives his life and is done. He does not continue the race with a line of children like himself. Because of his very low-grade condition, he never becomes a parent.'[84] (I should point out, as an aside, that by casting his 'idiot' as male, Goddard entirely sidesteps the possibility of an intellectually disabled woman becoming pregnant through the abusive actions of males of whatever grade of intelligence.) He notes that 'some have proposed the lethal chamber' as a solution to the problem of idiocy, but is confident that 'humanity is steadily tending away from the possibility of that method, and there is no probability that it will ever be practiced'.[85] What misplaced confidence.

For Goddard, the 'greatest problem' lay in the persons of the 'higher-grade' feeble-minded population whom he labelled 'morons', coining yet another word to add to the general armoury of intelligence-based insults, alongside 'idiot' and 'imbecile'. He saw Deborah as a typical example of 'the moron, the delinquent, the kind of girl or woman who fills our reformatories. They are wayward, they get into all sorts of trouble and difficulties, sexually and otherwise, and yet we have been unaccustomed to account for their defects on the basis of viciousness, environment, or ignorance.'[86] This is his conclusion of a brief account of Deborah's fourteen years at the Vineland School, which she had entered at the age of eight. Goddard believes her instructors have largely failed to educate her, and that any hopes they may have had for her improvement have been proved to have been wishful thinking. If the hope had been to make Deborah indistinguishable from any other young woman of her class and background, then there might be some justification for his pessimism. But just as the lost boy, Victor, emerges from Itard's account as a complex human being who has changed a great deal, Deborah confounds Goddard's attempt to reduce her to a symbol of defectiveness. 'The consensus of opinion' of the staff at the institution was that the young woman in the photograph

is cheerful, inclined to be quarrelsome, very active and restless, very affectionate, willing, and tries; is quick and excitable, fairly good-tempered. Learns a new occupation quickly, but requires a half hour or twenty-four repetitions to learn four lines. Retains well what she has once learned. Needs close supervision. Is bold towards strangers, kind towards animals. Can run an electric sewing machine, cook, and do practically everything about the house. Has no noticeable defect. She is quick and observing, has a good memory, writes fairly, does excellent work in wood-carving and kindergarten, is excellent in imitation. Is a poor reader and poor at numbers. Does fine basketry and gardening. Spelling is poor; music is excellent; sewing excellent; excellent in entertainment work. Very fond of children and good in helping care for them. Has a good sense of order and cleanliness. Is sometimes very stubborn and obstinate. Is not always truthful and has been known to steal, although does not have a reputation for this. Is proud of her clothes. Likes pretty dresses and likes to help in other cottages, even to temporarily taking charge of a group.[87]

In other words, Deborah had her strengths and her weaknesses, like anyone else. One plate in the book, entitled 'Specimens of Deborah's Handiwork', is made up of pictures of completed needlework and woodwork projects, including a beautifully embroidered doily, a dress, a wooden chest, a chair and what appear to be two small tables. To me, Deborah seems to have been accomplished, talented and eminently teachable. I find her needlework especially impressive, as my own needlework teacher at secondary school did not find me teachable at all.

Deborah's competencies were of little interest to Goddard – they didn't help him prove his point, which was that girls like her were a threat to 'racial hygiene'. In order to do this he needed to establish not only her feeble-mindedness, but its hereditary nature. Goddard employed fieldworkers to investigate the family histories of the Vineland residents. These were all women, not only because they would work for relatively little pay or credit, but also because Goddard believed that women's superior intuition would enable them to infer feeble-mindedness when they encountered it, from the speech and manner of the people they visited, and from the surroundings in which they found them. The fieldworker who investigated Deborah's family, Elizabeth S. Kite, is in fact credited in the preface to *The Kallikak Family*, and rightly so, as Goddard's conclusions rest entirely on the impressions she received when she visited Deborah's relatives, and on her ability to take the oral histories out of which she and Goddard would construct their genealogical story.

And what a story it was. Goddard chose the name 'Kallikak' because he believed he had identified two distinct branches of the family, one legitimate and upstanding, the other illegitimate and degenerate, both descended from the same man, Deborah's great-great-great-grandfather, whom Goddard named 'Martin Kallikak'. Before marriage, Martin had a liaison with a 'feeble-minded girl' he met at a tavern during the American Revolution, which resulted in a 'feeble-minded son' – Deborah's great-great-grandfather, also named Martin. Goddard states that 'from him have come four hundred and eighty descendants. One hundred and forty-three of these, we have conclusive proof, were or are feeble-minded, while only forty-six have been found normal.'[88] Among these descendants, his research has uncovered 'thirty-three sexually immoral persons, mostly prostitutes', 'twenty-four confirmed alcoholics' and eight who 'kept houses of ill fame'. These have married into other families 'generally of about the same type', producing further feeble-minded offspring.[89]

Goddard's aim is to prove that great evils might have been averted if only that attractive but feeble-minded tavern girl had been kept away from breeding stock. After Martin Kallikak abandoned her, he married a 'Quakeress' from a 'good' family, siring a legitimate line of Kallikaks, all of them successful, upstanding Americans. Both lines bore the same surname, allowing Kite and Goddard to discover their common ancestor and, in the contrasting stories of each group of descendants, a natural demonstration of the hereditary nature of feeble-mindedness. And perhaps they might have proved to be, if they had been true.

Deborah's real name was Emma Wolverton, and she seems to have suffered not so much from feeble-mindedness as from 'the consequences of poor decisions made by her mother'.[90] She was sent away on the insistence of a new stepfather and taken to Vineland. Her inability to get along with other children was taken as a sign of feeble-mindedness, so she spent the rest of her life in institutions, working as an unpaid domestic servant and teaching assistant. She was literate, well read and a great writer of letters. If she had any real difficulties, they were not intellectual so much as emotional and social – she had, at times, an explosive temper.

Emma was not Deborah, and the Wolvertons were not the Kallikaks. Later research showed that Emma's branch of the family included landowners, farmers, schoolteachers, the treasurer of a bank and a Second World War pilot; the other branch of the family, meanwhile, was discovered not to be 'free from troubles and human frailties'.[91] Any problems faced by Wolvertons on either side could be shown to be the consequence of the sort of social and economic misfortunes which any family might face. And Deborah's great-great-grandfather was not anybody's illegitimate son, but the legitimately born second cousin of the man Kite and Goddard had supposed to be his father. As Smith and Wehmeyer put it, 'Goddard's natural experiment never occurred'.[92]

That didn't stop the book's being a huge success. It remained in print until the end of the thirties, and was cited in psychology and biology textbooks as proof that feeble-mindedness was inherited. In 1927, it was used as evidence in the case of Buck v. Bell, which culminated in a Supreme Court ruling that the involuntary sterilization of 'mentally defective' persons was not unconstitutional in the United States. By 1938, thirty-three US states had passed laws allowing for the forced sterilization of women with learning disabilities and twenty-nine had made sterilization compulsory for people who were thought to have genetic conditions. Many European countries followed suit: Denmark in 1929, then Norway in 1934, and after that Sweden, Finland, Estonia, Iceland, Czechoslovakia, Yugoslavia, Latvia, Hungary and Turkey. The UK never had an official sterilization law, but it did happen in Britain, here and there.

What is the matter with you?
You are a diseased cell in the body politic.

In 1933, the Nazis came to power in your country, and it became a terrible place to be different in any way. Edith Sheffer explains this in the context of the German concept of *Gemüt* and its centrality to Nazi ideology. There's no direct translation into English, but it approximates to something like 'social spirit', the kind of 'community connectedness' (or, as I think of it, 'herd instinct') that does not come easily to people like us.

In the schools of the Third Reich, *Gemüt* was instilled into children from the earliest possible age. They learned that they were only to be valued as members of the larger national body, the clean, healthy and right-thinking *Volk*, from which problem individuals were to be rooted out like putrid matter.

What are we going to do with you?

The answer to this question was the Aktion T4 programme, named for the address of its central offices at Tiergartenstrasse No. 4 in Berlin. Hitler signed the order that set T4 in motion in October 1939, allowing German physicians to deliver a 'mercy death' to all German adults judged to be disabled or suffering from incurable diseases. Doctors had already been delivering death to children. The first to die was a five-month-old baby, Gerhard Kretschmar, born deaf and blind, with missing limbs, and diagnosed soon after with 'idiocy'. Gerhard's father wrote to Hitler requesting that his son be killed and Hitler ordered Karl Brandt, his personal physician, to examine the child. Brandt agreed with the diagnosis, and in October 1938 Gerhard was given a lethal injection at the clinic where he lived, during the nurses' coffee break.

It was not Gerhard's father who came up with the idea of so-called 'mercy death'. We know that it had been in the air for a good while, and not only in Germany. There is, for example, a distressing passage in Virginia Woolf's diary entry for 9 January 1915, describing a walk along the river:

> On the towpath we met & had to pass a long line of imbeciles. The first was a very tall young man, just queer enough to look twice at, but no more; the second shuffled, & looked aside; & then one realised that every one in that long line was a miserable ineffective shuffling idiotic

creature, with no forehead, or no chin, & an imbecile grin, or a wild suspicious stare. It was perfectly horrible. They should certainly be killed.[93]

In 1920 in Germany, Alfred Hoche and Karl Binding published their book *The Authorization for the Destruction of Life Unworthy of Life*. It is, I think, the origin of that phrase on your record – '*Lebensunwertes Leben!*' Hoche saw institutionalized people as analogous to ballast on a ship, using a term in common use: *Ballastexistenzen*. (Mel Baggs, responding defiantly to medical records which labelled them unsalvable, chose 'ballastexistenz' as the title of one of their blogs.)

Hoche and Binding's book, like Goddard's, proved very influential. In the summer following Gerhard's death, another of Hitler's physicians, Theo Morel, composed a document arguing for the need for a law to authorize 'Destruction of Life Unworthy of Life'. Morel stressed the economic benefits that would accrue from the elimination of these 'useless eaters'. In August 1939, it became compulsory for doctors and midwives to register all 'malformed' newborns. Their reports would be sent to a panel of three medical experts, who would decide whether a child should be sent to one of the new institutions which had been set up as killing wards. Condemned children were taken away in buses with darkened windows; a few weeks later, their parents would be sent letters informing them of their child's death, with cause and date altered. Many children were given lethal doses of medication, by tablet or injection, delivering a death which was usually neither quick nor painless; others were slowly starved to death. Despite the official lies, people understood what was happening. Local children knew enough to frighten each other with threats of buses.

As the programme moved on to adults, its officers began to experiment with ways of making the process more efficient. Grafeneck, where you were taken, was the first of six 'euthanasia' centres that came into operation in 1940 and 1941, before protests led to an end to this first, more organized phase of killing.

Records show that you arrived there on 25 June 1940. You were told to undress – or perhaps you had someone undress you, if you were unable to do this for yourself. You were given the quickest of physical examinations, and then moved with the other patients into a shed with sealed walls. Perhaps some of you became agitated at that point, in which case the staff would have calmed you down by explaining that you were there only to be given a shower, to be made clean. Then the doors were locked and poisonous gas was pumped in. You would have been unconscious within five minutes, and dead within ten. You must have been one of the first Jews – indeed, one of the first people – to be murdered this way. It was not because you were Jewish, but because you were disabled.

They took your life, Adelheid, but they did not erase your name or your memory. You are commemorated by a *Stolperstein*, or 'stumbling stone', set into the pavement outside your last family address on Döbelestraße in your hometown of Konstanz.

The stone's location and its inscription are detailed on the *Stolpersteine* website, alongside a brief biography and the name of your stone's 'godparent', Eyal Bloch.[94] Yes, that stone and your family honour your memory. When I contacted Eyal, I found out that he is an educationalist and social entrepreneur. He sent me one of his papers, 'Learning About, Learning From, Learning With: Emergence of a Social-Entrepreneurial Model of the Relations Between Society and People with Disabilities'. Its main argument is that individuals like you are people to be met, not problems to be solved. To have work like that done under the Bloch name – that's a legacy, isn't it? It is a *mitvah* indeed to write to you.

May your memory be a blessing.

Yours in love and sisterhood, always,
Joanne

Frau V

I have not found any dates for Frau V, or her real name. The little I know of her comes from the brief portrait which appears in the Austrian psychiatrist Hans Asperger's 1944 paper, '"Autistic Psychopathy" in childhood'. She was the mother of Fritz V, one of the troubled children who were brought to see Asperger when he was director of the Remedial Department at the University Paediatric Clinic in Vienna. For a long time, this paper was unknown in the English-speaking world. This changed in the eighties when the British-based psychologist Uta Frith translated the paper and another, Lorna Wing, took its author's name to create a new diagnosis – Asperger's Syndrome – which could be applied to individuals who showed autistic traits without evidence of language delay. This reflects the way in which the founding cohort of patients described by Asperger contrasted with those of Leo Kanner, the American-based Austrian émigré psychiatrist credited with first identifying autism in children. Broadly speaking, Kanner sees his young patients as merely defective; Asperger describes boys (entirely boys) who experience problems in many areas, but also believes them to have the potential for exceptional achievement. Asperger was working in Nazi-occupied Austria, and some have argued that he was a hero, emphasizing his patients' potential in order to save them from state-sanctioned murder. Others have questioned this, drawing attention to the number of children who passed through his clinic and on to the killing wards. Whether he resisted or collaborated, Asperger was working under conditions of murderous totalitarianism, which were especially hostile to any form of vulnerability or difference. Frau V had to mother under those same conditions: as a non-Jewish Austrian woman, her job was to bear and raise strong, disciplined and productive members of the German race. Unfortunately for her and for him, her eldest son didn't fit the mould. As Asperger tells it, neither did she. I don't know what became of her, whether or not she survived the war, and if she did, at what cost.

Letter to Frau V

Dear Frau V

Please forgive me, not only for writing out of the blue, but for everything. And I mean everything – everything you can possibly think of. Everything I meant to do. Everything I didn't mean to do. Everything I suspected was wrong. Everything I mistakenly believed to be right. And all the wrong things which, directly or indirectly, I caused other people to do. I'm a mother, and I have not put a foot right since the beginning of time.

You were a mother too – perhaps we might absolve each other?

Every mother is scrutinized and every mother is judged. The world in which your mothering was scrutinized was in many ways very different from mine, but there are significant similarities. We could both be described as white, middle-class, highly educated European women. Both of us, in becoming mothers, entered into a territory that was (and remains) the province of experts – midwives, health visitors, nurses, doctors, educationalists, psychologists and social workers. Often state-appointed, they patrol the boundaries of normative child development, ready to take action if any child, or mother, or family shows signs of straying outside.

My own mother, a social worker involved in child protection, explained this to me when I was still a teenager: *We're society's soft policemen*, she said. Sometimes actual policemen get involved too. And, as non-experts, we are expected to scrutinize each other and, if necessary, tip off the experts. Even in this supposedly free society, there's something authoritarian about the state of modern motherhood.

This is where our conditions diverge, and sharply. You were not mothering in a free society. You were living in Nazi-occupied Vienna, and it is hard to imagine a more dangerous place in which to stray outside the norm. In a society where nothing was more important than *Gemüt* – social spirit, a sense of oneself as a member of the *Volk* – you were raising Fritz, a *Gemüt*-deficient son.

In the autumn of 1939, your Fritz was six years old, and his lack of *Gemüt* was getting him into trouble at school. He was referred to the Heilpadagogiche Abteiling (Remedial Department, or Curative Education Department) of the University Paediatric Clinic in Vienna, where he was assessed by Hans Asperger and his team. As Asperger would write in his paper on 'autistic psychopathy' five years later, Fritz

was never able to become integrated into a group of playing children. He never got on with other children and, in fact, was not interested in them. They only 'wound him up'. He quickly became aggressive and lashed out with anything he could get hold of (once with a hammer), regardless of the danger to others. For this he was thrown out of kindergarten after only a few days. Similarly, because of his totally uninhibited behaviour, his schooling failed on the first day. He had attacked other children, walked nonchalantly about in class and tried to demolish the coat-racks.[95]

From an early age, his behaviour had been just as challenging at home. He had no respect for adult authority, would not do as he was told, broke things and exhibited only occasional, abrupt 'fits' of affection towards his family and others.

Presumably, as Fritz's mother, you were Asperger's main informant. You appear to have been a good and thorough one. Asperger describes you as a mother who 'knew her son through and through and understood his difficulties very well'. It sounds as if you might well have had a good deal of empathy for your boy, even though you were 'not coping' with your son's 'physical care' and 'emphasized again and again' that you were 'at the end of [your] tether', something which was obvious to Asperger as soon as he saw the two of you together.[96]

Your inability to cope was not the only thing that Asperger found striking about you. As he wrote under the heading 'Family History':

> The mother herself was very similar to the boy. This similarity was particularly striking given that she was a woman, since, in general, one would expect a higher degree of intuitive social adaptation in women, more emotion than intellect.[97]

Asperger certainly expected better 'intuition' in women; he usually found it. Like the eighteenth-century French physician Itard, who had depended on Mme Guerin to socialize his 'wild boy' subject Victor, Asperger was supported at the clinic by a team of female nurses who, between examinations and sessions of formal instruction, cared for the children who resided there.

It is Asperger's name on the paper, and Asperger who gave his name to the sub-type of autism with which I would be diagnosed in 2012, but much of the work of the Curative Education clinic was organized under the leadership of its head nurse, Victorine Zak. Zak was in charge for thirty years, and during that time she developed theories and honed open-ended, play-centred therapeutic techniques that are still in use today.[98] Behind her work was a carefully thought-out philosophy, tried and tested in the clinic, which she set out in a series of articles published for *The International Council of Nurses*. To have developed and described her techniques in such a way that they could be passed on, Zak must have possessed considerable intelligence of the systematic kind, but she envisaged her own work in terms of what we now call emotional intelligence, stating that the clinic's aim was to 'experience the child's thought process empathically'.[99] Asperger agreed, calling her 'the soul of the ward', and waxing lyrical on the way in which her 'thoroughly feminine powers' served to 'guide the male intellect'.[100]

Zak, you see, was 'motherly', just as she ought to have been, just as anyone would have expected a woman to be. You, on the other hand, had a far lower degree of 'intuitive social adaptation' than Asperger would have expected in a woman. Like your son, you appear to have been somewhat lacking in *Gemüt*. Asperger writes this of you: 'In the way she moved and spoke, indeed in her whole demeanour, she seemed strange and rather a loner.' This seems to have been obvious from the moment you and Fritz entered the hospital:

> Very characteristic, for instance, was the situation when mother and son walked to the hospital school together, but each by themselves. The mother slouched along, hands held behind back and apparently oblivious to the world. Beside her the boy was rushing to and fro, doing mischief.

They gave the appearance of having absolutely nothing to do with each other.[101]

It occurs to me, reading this, that in not forcing interaction or physical closeness onto a boy who would not have wanted it, you might have been displaying what Asperger acknowledged to be a sound understanding of your son.

You recognized the similarities between yourself and Fritz, and between Fritz and other members of your family, finding 'similar traits' in yourself and your relations, and talking 'eloquently' on the subject. However, your understanding of your son was not in itself enough to enable you to cope with his difficulties. Asperger thought that the crisis which had brought you to his clinic was clearly 'due not only to the boy's own internally caused problems, but also to the mother's own problems in relating to the outside world, showing as she did a limited intuitive social understanding'. Moreover, he could not help thinking 'that the mother found it difficult to cope not only with her child but with the practical matters of life. She was certainly not up to running the household. Even living, as she did, in the upper echelons of society, she always looked unkempt, unwashed almost, and was always badly dressed.' When you felt overwhelmed at home, you would apparently 'walk out' on your family and go to the mountains you loved for a week or more, leaving the family to 'struggle for themselves'.[102]

Given that you were living in the 'upper echelons', I am wondering how much you would have had to do with your children's upbringing in any case; I'm assuming that the 'family' who struggled without you included the servants who would have taken care of the day-to-day running of your household, even if they were supposed to do so under your direction. I cannot imagine that you were Fritz's only caregiver, or the only influence on his life and upbringing, although Asperger does not seem to have asked you about any others. He also has relatively little to say about Fritz's father. After describing your shortcomings as a woman and mother for several paragraphs, he has only this to say about Fritz's father, a high-ranking civil servant from an 'ordinary farming family, with no reported peculiarities':

> He married late and was fifty-five years old when his first child was born. The father was a withdrawn and reticent man who did not give much away about himself. He clearly hated to talk about himself and his interests. He was extremely correct and pedantic and kept a more than usual distance.[103]

You husband was apparently not as good an informant as you were; you appear to have been honest about yourself and your situation and generous with details. In your thoroughness I see not only desperation, but also your commitment to helping your son. It doesn't sound as if your husband was able to give you much in the way of support, but I suppose, then as now, much less was expected of fathers.

If fathers had accompanied their children to more expert appointments over the last century, and been more forthcoming in consulting rooms, perhaps the experts would have had more to say about the effect of fathers on their children. It's an irony that, by being such a good and conscientious historian of your own life and your child's, you were giving Asperger all the more material with which to judge you. And judge he does, passing critical comments on your appearance, your demeanour, your social skills, your housekeeping, your desire to spend time by yourself, your general unwomanliness. You are more like your son than you are like Sister Zak, and really it ought to be the other way round. And so he judges you. What he does not do, despite the striking resemblance to your son, is suggest that, as a child, you might have shared your son's diagnosis.

You could be forgiven for finding this surprising. Elsewhere in the paper, under 'Genetic and Biological Factors', Asperger writes: 'The idea that psychopathic states [which is what autism was understood to be at the time] are constitutional and, hence, inheritable has long been confirmed.'[104] While he recognizes that the genetic picture is complex, and admits that he has not traced the pedigree of his patients, as many clinicians did under the Nazis,[105] he states quite clearly that he and his team 'have been able to discern related incipient traits in parents or relatives, in *every* single case where it was possible for us to make a closer acquaintance'. Often they also found 'the fully fledged autistic picture'.[106] Up until this point, Asperger has remained on the fence as to the typical gender and class aspects of this picture, but now he starts talking about fathers, and not just any kind of father – fathers with 'intellectual professions'. Exceptions to class and profession can be shrugged off as '[if] one happens to find a manual worker among them, then it is probably someone who has missed his vocation'. Here he directs the reader to a case history featuring such a father, and I might have expected him to allude to you as an analogous exception to the upper-class male rule, but he does not. He does not mention you directly at all. Instead, he writes:

It is fascinating to note that the autistic children we have seen are almost exclusively *boys*. Sometimes girls had contact disturbances which were reminiscent of autism, and there were also girls in whom a preceding encephalitis[107] had caused the state... However, we never found the fully formed picture... How can this be explained? There is a strong hint at a sex-linked or at least sex-limited mode of inheritance.

And so we come to this confident statement: 'The autistic personality is an extreme variant of male intelligence.'[108]

Asperger put these three words together – autistic, male, intelligent – and never thought to question the cultural assumptions or prejudices which made them seem so obviously inextricable. When I was first thinking about writing to you, I read a book by Edith Sheffer called *Asperger's Children: The Origins of Autism in Nazi Vienna*. She devotes a whole chapter to examining the way in which these assumptions and prejudices about class and gender coloured Asperger's clinical judgement. (If you ask me, it doesn't matter how scientific and objective a researcher means to be; when one person is looking at another person, assumptions will always get in the way – assumptions, and inequalities. And, in case it isn't obvious, you can add age, race, sexuality and disability to the list.)

One thing is pretty obvious to Sheffer, as it is to me: Asperger was not terribly interested in girls, clinically or intellectually. The meat of Asperger's paper lies in its four case histories: three meticulously detailed examples of boys with 'autistic psychopathy' and one briefer study of a fourth boy, Hellmuth L, the fourth child of parents 'without any peculiarities', whose autistic symptoms have arisen from brain damage. (So that's Frau L off the hook.) You might think from this that there were very few girls at the clinic, but you would be wrong. Sheffer takes three girls – Christine, Margarete and Elfriede – and recreates three more case histories to stand alongside Asperger's studies of Harro, Ernst and your boy. These girls were differentiated from the male trio not only by gender, but also by their family circumstances and their age on admission to the clinic. While the boys arrived before puberty, came from conventional two-parent homes, and were referred by their schools, the girls were all in their teens, and were referred by welfare officers; Christine did not get on with her stepmother, Margarete's father was in jail, and Elfriede had been born out of wedlock.

Despite the clear differences between the children's backgrounds, Sheffer is able to draw out some equally clear similarities in their behaviour. All six of them have arrived at the Curative Education ward because of their difficult or 'anti-social' behaviour – what they share is a deficiency of *Gemüt*. Your Fritz is 'wound up' by other children. Christine is described as 'constantly a loner and pensive', a girl who cannot forge relationships with the other evacuees in her camp, who is even 'vindictive to her comrades'. Harro has been 'referred... by his school as unmanageable', after talking back to his teacher and displaying a 'savage tendency to fight'.[109] Margarete has 'impossible conduct at home': she is 'cheeky' to her mother, will not help with the housework and repeatedly runs away.[110] Ernst cannot go to the park without 'instantly get[ting] embroiled in fighting',[111] while Elfriede, like Margarete, is an inveterate runaway, whose behaviour in general is considered to be both troublesome and highly inappropriate.

For Asperger, a disturbance in social relationships, in *Gemüt*, is the defining characteristic of 'autistic psychopathy'. If this were the only significant criterion, one might expect Christine, Margarete and Elfriede to receive the same diagnosis as Fritz, Harro and Ernst, but this doesn't happen. The boys' difficult behaviour, however 'malicious', while not precisely excused, is read again and again as a confirmatory sign of their unusual and intriguing pathology. The girls' behaviour, on the face of it, is far less disruptive: they are portrayed as uncooperative and quarrelsome rather than violent, and if they pose any physical risk, it is only to themselves. None of this matters, though, because their behaviour is not interesting, either to the researchers who assess them or the staff who care for them. Their bad behaviour is a predictable accompaniment to the arrival of puberty and menstruation, which is distasteful, but not interesting. The peculiarities of the boys' language are taken to be indicative of a rare and original kind of intelligence, and some of their stranger utterances are quoted and examined at some length in Asperger's paper, but there doesn't seem to be anything the girls can say or write that can provoke anything other than weariness and contempt.

What the girls often expressed was anxiety, about why they were in the clinic, how long they might stay, and where they might go afterwards. This was entirely warranted. Take Margarete, for example. The first of her two stays was a brief one: she arrived in August, was quickly judged to be 'in danger of waywardness (deceit, abnormal embarrassing acts, and staying out for hours)', and before September was out, she had been transferred to Spiegelgrund, a clinic whose staff had the state-sanctioned task of murdering patients considered to be unworthy of care. Although the doctors at Spiegelgrund decided that Margarete required 'permanent stay in a mental institution', and referred her to Steinhof, which specialized in murdering adults, she managed to survive both killing centres and was discharged in October 1942. Now fifteen, Margarete proved herself to be a productive citizen, finding work in a factory, but outside working hours she continued to get into trouble, stealing from her mother and 'hanging around with soldiers'. By the end of that year, another psychiatrist had assessed her as unlikely to be able to learn or to work and recommended her transfer to Pavilion 17 at Spiegelgrund, where he might well have expected her story to end. Remarkably, though, the chief physician in Pavilion 17 disagreed with Margarete's most recent assessments, and even believed that she was 'tentatively educable'.[112] He sent her home.

In April 1944, Margarete was back at Asperger's clinic, telling her extraordinary story to the nurse who was supervising her bath. The nurse noted that Margarete was 'very talkative', speaking 'a lot' about her life, and giving what you would imagine to be a harrowing account of her time in various institutions. The nurse, however, seems to have been bored by Margarete's story, and irritated by the way in which she told it: 'In questioning about her crimes, she reports a lot of trivialities in detail, but not the essentials. It puts the listener's patience to the test. One is happy when she is finished.'[113] It may be that, like Fritz or Harro or Ernst, Margarete was exhibiting a deficiency in the 'contact-creating expressive functions' which Asperger saw as so typical of autistic patients, and this was why the nurse could not warm to her. The reference to detailed 'trivialities' also suggests that Margarete's account had something of that exhaustive quality that often characterizes the spoken communication of autistic people – me included. But apparently her language was not interesting, not even clinically. That alone might have been enough to kill her, but this time the staff judged her able to work, and she was released.

Elfriede also survived, despite the fact that, like Margarete, she was sent to Spiegelgrund. Christine, whom Asperger found 'hateful in many situations', was sent to Theresienfeld reformatory. When the staff there tried to send her home ten months later, Asperger would not allow it. While Asperger and his staff went to considerable lengths to test the intelligence of the three uncooperative boys, no such attempts are recorded in the girls' records. They were girls and it was their lack of 'intuitive social adaptation' that mattered. When I look back over Asperger's description of you, I do not get the sense that intellectual ability was considered to be much of a mitigating factor in a woman, although it undoubtedly was for your son. You could not do what was expected of you as a wife and a mother; you did not comport yourself as a woman should, and neither did those three girls – that was the point. That was the only point.

What drew me to you in the first place was the way in which you keep defiantly being a person in your own right, when Asperger's interest in you is only as Fritz's mother. The image that stays with me is of you, alone, walking in your 'beloved' mountains, un-defined by your relationships. It's perfectly possible for a person to define herself without reference to her relationships. The canoni-cal Western philosophers I studied at university did this as a matter of course: there are no transitive verbs in 'I think, therefore I am'. There is no acknowledgement, in Descartes' self-sufficient formulation, that we need other people to bring us into the world to think, other people to keep us fed and safe while we grow up and develop our thinking capacities, other people to educate us so that we can use them effectively, and, in the end, other people to care for us in our last days, to bury us, and to remember what we said about thinking after we're gone. And in between those two most dependent stages, our sense of ourselves as independent beings can only be maintained through a determined and per-sistent forgetting of the innumerable ways in which we continue to depend on the efforts of others throughout our lives. Who fetched the wood or coal for the fire in Descartes' hearth? Who made the chair he sat on? Who cleaned it? Who made and laundered the shift he was wearing while he wrote? Who bought and prepared the food his body was busily transforming into thinking and writing energy? Who made the ink? The paper?

I know that I'm mixing up many different kinds of dependency here. Many of the relationships we depend upon are explicitly contractual, and it seems to be generally understood that when you pay for someone else's efforts you also pay for the right not to have to think about what it might cost that person to make those efforts. And you don't have to pay them very much either. (I should add that the ongoing Covid-19 emergency has made the efforts of care workers, food retail workers, cleaners, delivery workers and others starkly visible, and with it the extent of our dependence on them. Whether this new appreciation outlasts the immediate crisis remains to be seen. If it does, decent pay might be a good start.)

The way we depend on our mothers is different: there is no contract, and we don't reimburse them. At the same time, we are not routinely in the habit of thinking about our mothers as people-in-themselves any more than we are in the habit of speculating on the interiority of the people who drive our trains, clean our offices, take our money in shops or book our doctors' appointments. Unless we make a conscious effort to *see* them, all we notice routinely is whether they provide for our needs in a way that doesn't inconvenience or frustrate us (and of course structural inequalities in gender, class and race can exacerbate this not-seeing). It is in this respect, in the way that the dependency only becomes visible when disrupted, that the two kinds of relationship are very much the same. We don't ordinarily acknowledge mothers as whole and separate persons. So it's little wonder that, when you needed to assert your personhood, you had to leave off mothering for a bit, and climb up a mountain. To paraphrase Descartes: If I can't hear myself think, how am I supposed to know that I am?

I mother, therefore I'm not. The psychoanalyst D. W. Winnicott, who came up with the merciful concept of the 'good-enough mother', also developed the trickier notion of the mother as 'holding environment'. In the earliest days of an infant's life, according to Winnicott, its well-being and development depend upon the mother's ability to tune into her child at the expense of everything else, including her own sense of separate personhood. This tuning in should, in time, allow her to recognize when the infant is ready to move beyond this benign illusion that baby and mother and world are all one and the same. Then the good-enough mother can begin to respond to the infant's tentative assertions of its own separateness in such a way that the infant will come to understand that self and environment are two separate things, which it cannot expect to be always in perfect accord. Winnicott trusted that a good-enough mother, if supported by those around her, would be able to facilitate this complex and delicate procedure without having read his books first.

So far, so good-enough, but what if you are among the not-good-enough? It's one thing not to be perfect, but not even to be good-enough? The good-enough mother stands in the same relation to the perfect mother as the normal does to the ideal: it promises to represent a realistic and not-too-punishing aspiration, but it is more perilous to find yourself outside the normal than it is to fail to meet an ideal. Descriptions of what is normal have a way of becoming prescriptions. I read Winnicott's work before I came to be a mother, and I took it very much to heart. I read quite a few other psychoanalytic texts on early infancy and the mother, and took a lot of them to heart too.

To give one example, I can still just about remember Wilfred Bion's alpha-function. 'Alpha-function' is his term for the operation the psyche has to perform in order to process experience and sense impressions as they come in from the outside; to maintain a psyche that is capable of continually refashioning itself in response to that experience, without descending into incoherence. According to Bion, we are not born with it, and during early infancy the mother has to perform this function for the infant. If she can't, the consequences will require therapy. Occasionally this or that therapist would suggest, in simpler language, that my own mother's capacity to facilitate alpha-function must have been in some way impaired, so I saw myself as living proof.

That may not be a very accurate rendering of Bion's theory, but it's a reasonable facsimile of the version I had in my head as I entered motherhood. I was concerned that I hadn't had enough therapy to exorcize my inherited neuroses and prevent them from possessing the baby. I was worried about the possible effects of my worrying. I've told my early-motherhood story before, but not to you, so here's a short-ish version. By the time I got pregnant, I had already been diagnosed with depression and anxiety, and had been taking medication, on and off, for several years. I came off the medication when I was trying to conceive, which I managed to do quite quickly. That first conception resulted in a long-drawn-out and traumatic miscarriage, which left me anaemic, grief-stricken and full of guilt: I had failed, in a very concrete way, to provide a maternal environment for that first foetus. I was obsessed with getting pregnant again. I got my way quite quickly, before I'd given myself a chance to address the trauma of my previous agonizing, haemorrhaging baby loss.

So I carried that into the next pregnancy, which, apart from symphysis pubis dysfunction and carpal tunnel syndrome, was pretty straightforward – if you also discount the fact that I went mad.

It's actually quite easy to go mad when you're pregnant. The culture around pregnancy is already mad: when I alluded to authoritarianism earlier, I was thinking mainly of pregnancy and early motherhood, when the state and its agents bombard you with advice, and then surveil you to make sure you are following it. Your distance from the norm, along with your infant's distance from it, are tracked through hundreds of tiny measurements, recorded on computers but also in little books, which you are expected to look after yourself. And if that wasn't maddening enough, the powers-that-be keep changing everything, contradicting their advice and moving the norm around, seemingly at will. It's no surprise that I went mad; it's only surprising that more women don't.

It was a kind of health-and-safety madness. I've since learned to call it obsessive compulsive disorder (OCD), but at the time, all I knew was that I had to keep my baby and my baby's flesh container – me – safe, and that the responsibility seemed overwhelming. There were so many hazards to consider: cars that might hit me, bicycles that might hit me, people that might also knock me over, if they ran into me with sufficient force; there were undercooked foods, unpasteurized foods (see also glasses of unsterilized water that might have been left out too long), prepared foods that could harbour bacteria, and any kind of food at all might choke me; there were bodies of water to fall into – including the bath, if I slipped; there was a rapist on the news; there were flights of stairs to fall down.

Oh God, the stairs. I was especially concerned by the stairs that went from the first floor of our house to my study in the loft: they were steep and narrow, and a builder had told us they were not fire-proof. My study was cold, and I would work with an electric heater next to me. It occurred to me that it might be possible for the heater to get too hot, and cause something to catch fire – a wooden desk, a book, a sheet of paper – which would in turn cause a sheet of flame to block my exit. All might not be lost, though: there was a wooden desk underneath the single, small casement window, which gave out onto the bathroom roof. Every time I imagined the fire scenario – which was often – I would imagine the escape scenario in the hope of countering it, and making the fear go away. But it never worked. In the end, around the fifteenth or sixteenth week of pregnancy, I caught myself taking it one step further and actually trying to haul myself, bump and all, onto the table. At that moment I realized I needed help, and not with fire safety. I confessed to my doctor; she put me on citalopram and the fires in my head died down a little.

The pregnancy continued. My obsessiveness took a calmer, more studious form. We took two birthing classes and my hand was always up at both of them. I bought a birthing ball and did pre-natal exercises with it that were designed to get the baby into the best position. To the same end, I slept on my left side. I bought re-useable nappies. I attended the local breastfeeding workshop and refused to buy a single item of bottle-feeding paraphernalia. I was going to birth my child with the least possible medical interference, because evidence showed that that was best for mother and baby. Then I was going to spend at least a year as a full-time mother – no paid help, no nursery, no competing commitments – and I was going to breastfeed all the way through. It would be a new start with a new person, an opportunity to get something right – or, at least, right enough.

At thirty-nine-and-a-half weeks, I went into labour, timed the contractions until they were five minutes apart and went into hospital, where I failed to progress because my baby was in the worst possible position, and wound up having an emergency C-section. I had relatively little trouble accepting that. But then I could not breastfeed, and that I could not accept at all. How could I, when everything I'd read or heard had shown me that only breastfeeding could give my new son exactly what he needed, enable a proper mother–baby bond, pass on my antibodies and reduce my chance of breast cancer? Unfortunately, no one had told my son, who arrived with dangerously low blood sugar and had to be given supplement before my milk had come in. Neither had anyone told my thyroid, which gave out at some point in the pregnancy, wrecked my metabolism and turned my milk to sugar water. After three months, I gave up trying to breastfeed. Two months later, my GP realized I had a goitre, and I was diagnosed with severe hypothyroidism. I realized that the exhaustion I'd been suffering from was more than the tiredness of early parenthood – I was seriously ill. We were so lucky to be able to pay a part-time nanny to help me at that point. I don't know where we might have wound up if we hadn't been (and I don't know why, in this day and age, in an affluent country like ours, childcare isn't affordable for everybody who needs it, whether this is because they are in paid work, or because they are, as I was, too ill to manage). Then, when my son was eighteen months old and going to the crèche at my husband's workplace part-time, I was diagnosed with OCD and was given further, voluntary help. Biologically, psychologically, I was anything but good enough.

God, the *judging* – of oneself, and the fear of it, from other mothers. You become so sensitive that you sense judgement pending even when it isn't there. I assumed that any mother who could breastfeed was judging me because I couldn't. It remains a painful issue for me, and not only for me; recently I read the following review of a book in which I'd written an account of living with OCD: 'I did find this book brilliant. Up until the comment about mothers who choose to bottle-feed. Us mothers who choose to bottle-feed should not be made to feel inferior. I have enough of feeling inferior with my ocd.' By writing about my struggle not to bottle-feed, I'd managed to make a woman who'd chosen bottle-feeding feel judged. I honestly didn't mean to, and I feel bad that I did, but I can see now that it was probably unavoidable. Where there's mothering, there's guilt and judgement; guilt, judgement and shame.

I started that book with a chapter about shame. I wanted to explain how shame is less about doing wrong – that's guilt – than it is about *being* wrong. Since I first wrote about it, 'shaming' has become a word that you hitch to nouns, as in: slut-shaming, fat-shaming, body-shaming etc. I'd like to add 'frump-shaming' to that list – it's what Asperger was doing when he criticized your less-than-immaculate appearance. He 'mum-shamed' you too: 'mum-shaming' is what we do to mothers when we shame them for the way they mother their children. It's what I inadvertently did to that reviewer of my book.

Guilt attaches to an act, but shame attaches to a person. I'd made that woman feel as if she were the wrong sort of mother. The quintessential right sort of mother is the breastfeeding Madonna, divinely graced with her motherly and 'thoroughly feminine powers', naturally and thoughtlessly allowing her substance to flow into her baby, who is her living complement, her context and her meaning. And if you feel at any point that it isn't coming naturally – the milk or the mothering – that you need to *think* about it, that you're having to *try*, that you actually might need *help* from another person, well then you are not the right sort of mother.

*

It's impossible to talk about the cultural history of autism without talking about mum-shaming. Asperger may have been the first to mum-shame, but he was far from being the worst. While Asperger was observing certain traits in your son in Vienna, Leo Kanner was observing similar traits in a group of children at his clinic in Baltimore. In 1943, he published his findings in a paper called 'Autistic Disturbances of Affective Contact'. This would go on to be one of the most cited papers in the history of child psychiatry. I think it would be fair to say that, before Uta Frith and Lorna Wing introduced Asperger's work to an Anglophone readership in the eighties, it was regarded as the unchallenged founding text of autism in most of the world. Unlike Asperger, Kanner did not consider the children he studied to have any significant intellectual or artistic potential, but he shared Asperger's tendency to mum-shame.

If you want evidence, there's plenty of it in a paper Kanner wrote in 1948: 'Problems of Nosology and Psychodynamics of Early Infantile Autism'. I want to stop and look at that title for a moment. The word 'nosology' refers to the classification of diseases: mental disorders, like bacterial disorders, flora and fauna, are treated as distinct kinds; in order to become intelligible, they must be appropriately placed in a taxonomic system. Knowledge isn't knowledge unless it can be sorted neatly. With this exact and scientific hinterland, 'nosology' seems to me to sit rather uncomfortably next to 'psychodynamics', which is an altogether more slippery kind of word. Here's a definition of psychodynamic therapy from an online medical dictionary: 'Psychodynamic therapy is based on the assumption that a person is having emotional problems because of unresolved, generally unconscious conflicts, often stemming from childhood.'[114]

'Psychodynamics' refers to 'emotional problems' which arise from 'conflicts, often stemming from childhood'. 'Emotional problems', unlike flora and fauna, are not directly perceptible; neither are internal 'conflicts'. You can only infer them, along with the childhood events that caused them, and that inference only makes sense in relation to a shared set of assumptions that cannot themselves be directly proved. The first word, 'nosology', seems to imply that Kanner's observations and analysis in the paper rest on some kind of scientific method, but I don't see how anyone could acquire knowledge about psychodynamics by scientific means. I'm not saying the concept isn't in any way useful; I'm just saying it isn't scientific. It has no business pretending it belongs in the same discipline as 'nosology'.

That's what I think. Let's say that you're not me, though. Let's say you are someone who believes that you can infer the existence of 'conflicts', even if they are 'unconscious', and show that they are often 'stemming from childhood'. Someone like Leo Kanner, who learned to be a psychiatrist at a time when the discipline was heavily influenced by psychoanalytic ideas. Kanner was working in the same broad tradition as Bion and Winnicott; he looked at the child; he looked at the mother; he looked from one to the other, and he looked back again. He pushed aside the question of heredity for the time being (although he did acknowledge its significance elsewhere), and he made the first of his observations:

All but five of the mothers of the 55 children have attended college. All but one have been active vocationally before, and some also after, marriage as scientists, laboratory technicians, nurses, physicians, librarians, or artists.[115]

So, Kanner's mothers were, like you, educated and accomplished women; unlike you, but like most mothers today, they had established identities as working women before they had their children. (It is worth remembering that this was during the Second World War, when women of all classes were expected to work in order to support the war effort.) He remarks that his 'search for autistic children of unsophisticated parents has remained unsuccessful to date'. (I would question how hard he looked.) This has led him to speculate about a 'possible relationship' between the personalities, attitudes and approaches to parenting which these 'sophisticated' parents share and their children's similar 'psychopathologic manifestations'.[116]

To Kanner, it seems that these mothers take a rather cerebral and systematic approach to motherhood; they are not the kind of naturally intuitive mothers required to facilitate the healthiest infant development. Instead, they share with their husbands what Kanner 'should like to call a mechanization of human relationships'.[117] This shared approach results in marriages which he describes as undemonstrative, but respectful, and noticeably successful. You might think from this acknowledgement that something might be learned from this unusual mode of relating, but you would be wrong. Doubly so, where child-rearing is concerned:

> The parents' behavior toward the children must be seen to be fully appreciated. Maternal lack of genuine warmth is often conspicuous in the first visit to the clinic... I saw only one mother of an autistic child who proceeded to embrace him warmly and bring her face close to his.[118]

It never occurs to him, as it never occurred to Asperger, that perhaps the mothers didn't embrace their children, or bring their faces close to theirs, because they knew their children well enough to realize that they wouldn't like it if they did. (My own mother remembered me as a baby who didn't want to be cuddled very much, and that was something she learned to respect. I'm grateful to her for that.) Instead, he continues to elaborate on his picture of these overthinking, underfeeling, unnatural parents: 'Many of the fathers and most of the mothers are perfectionists. Obsessive adherence to set rules serves as a substitute for the enjoyment of life.'[119] They do not seem to him to be able to 'derive enjoyment from the children as they are'; rather than loving their children unconditionally, they 'work for the attainment of goodness, obedience, quiet, good eating, earliest possible control of elimination, large vocabularies, memory feats'.[120] The mothers 'felt duty-bound to carry out to the letter the rules and regulations which they were given by their obstetricians and pediatricians. They were anxious to do a good job, and this meant mechanized service of the kind which is rendered by an overconscientious gasoline station attendant.'[121] Kanner mothers exhibit 'impersonal, mechanized relation with the children'; they are like mechanics, and approach their children as if they were machines. So like machines, and so close to machines, they are in danger of becoming machines, domestic machines; when it happens, it feels inevitable:

These people, who themselves had been reared sternly in EMOTIONAL REFRIGERATORS [my capitals], have found at an early age that they could gain approval only through unconditional surrender to standards of perfection.[122]

And so, in turn, most of Kanner's child patients 'were exposed from the beginning to parental coldness, obsessiveness, and a mechanical type of attention to material needs only... THEY WERE KEPT NEATLY IN REFRIGERATORS WHICH DID NOT DEFROST.'[123]

With that, the Refrigerator Mother (not parent, just mother) came into being, and she would remain at the centre of the discourse around autism, dispensing mum-shame and mother-blame in all directions, for far, far too long.

As I've only met you, and Kanner's mothers, as characters constructed by psychiatrists, I wouldn't care to speculate about the emotional temperature of your mothering; it would be entirely unfair to do so. When it comes to the clinicians' attitudes towards the mothers of their patients, I feel no such compunction. They clearly didn't warm to you or to your American sisters. The mothers are not the refrigerators: the mothers are *in* the refrigerators.

Asperger and Kanner would have been on the alert for faults, so it's no surprise that they found them. I've suggested that your apparent lack of affection towards Fritz could be interpreted as respect for his need for his own space, and that the same could apply to Kanner's mothers. Another noticeable parallel between your behaviour and theirs is that, like you, the Kanner mothers are thorough and conscientious historians of their children's development. Asperger identifies you as a mother who 'knew her son through and through and understood his difficulties very well. She tried to find similar traits in herself and in her relations and talked about this eloquently.'[124] To give Asperger his due, he seems to value your eloquence and insight, although elsewhere he comments that the way you speak was 'strange'. Kanner also acknowledges that 'the obsessiveness of the parents of the autistic children was a veritable boon to me with regard to the case histories'.[125] A sign of a good parent, then? No, not at all, because this same 'obsessiveness was a major contribution to the impersonal, mechanized relation with the children'.[126]

A few years ago, not long after I received my own autism diagnosis, I was recruited as a member of an advisory panel to help design a study on the experiences of autistic mothers. I was one of six mothers on the panel; I could be misremembering, but I might have been the only one who was not also the mother of at least one autistic child. It's not uncommon for late-diagnosed autistic women to have received their own diagnoses as an unexpected consequence of going through the process for their children. I'm relatively unusual in that it didn't happen that way for me.

I remember that much of that first conversation centred on the difficulties of getting their autistic children's diagnoses recognized and their needs met. I had nothing to add to that specifically, but I could identify with the other women's struggles to make themselves understood by professionals, and their sense that they themselves were objects of curiosity, and often of suspicion. It seemed to all of us that there was a way to perform motherhood properly in the consulting room, and that we weren't able to do it. What we saw as conscientious and helpful – doing our research, making suggestions, acquiring the correct clinical terms – was seen by professionals as odd, inappropriate and uncooperative.

Sometimes this obsessive eloquence (to borrow a term each from Kanner and Asperger) strikes the professionals as an indication of something potentially dangerous, and the mother is suspected of making up her child's illness to get the drama and attention she craves for herself. Reporting on the results of the study in a conference paper, the researchers note that: 'Allegations of fabricated illness,[127] and high rates of surveillance by social services suggest there may be discrimination towards mothers with autism.'[128] Interviewed for a *Guardian* article profiling four autistic mothers, Dr Judith Gould said: '[The mothers'] own autism, often undiagnosed, means they put professionals' backs up and can be accused of causing or fabricating their children's condition'.[129] One of the mothers interviewed for the article, Melanie Mahjenta, was herself accused of fabricating illness by paediatricians and social services, as she struggled to get her three-year-old daughter Rosie diagnosed with autism. As she explained,

'Rosie was incorrectly diagnosed as not being autistic in 2013, despite the results from a clinical assessment which found she was on the spectrum,' says Melanie. 'I believe the team rejected the assessment results because they had a basic lack of understanding about the different manifestations of autism, particularly in females. They refused me a second opinion, which is unlawful, and accused me of fabricating Rosie's symptoms.

'The team also failed to recognise that I was on the autistic spectrum, although I told them that I believed I was. They should have been able to recognise my behaviour – which I understand can be challenging – as typical of an autistic parent.

Mahjenta believes that although her autism made her situation more complicated, it did, in the end, prove an advantage in the fight for her daughter's interests:

'When Rosie was made a child in need, my friends and family told me to stop fighting for her diagnosis. But I couldn't stop: part of being autistic is being unable to cope with injustice.

'I understand that my autism makes me a difficult person to deal with: I don't know when to back off when I know I'm right. Maybe I can't always look people in the eye, so perhaps I come over as being shifty. Autistic people do hyper-focus, but they mistook my obsession as a sign I was unstable.

'But although those traits are hard for people to deal with, my autism was ultimately a good thing. Perhaps a neurotypical person would have thought the doctor knew best and backed off. Or they would have stopped fighting because they feared losing their child. But I fought on and because of that, not only has Rosie finally been diagnosed with autism, opening the doors for more support, but the ombudsman found in my favour on all my points, and even awarded us damages.'

I've been fortunate enough to have been spared those kinds of experiences, perhaps because my own child is not autistic, but I can certainly recall occasions when my own penchant for using what I thought was the correct term got me slapped down. My son went through a phase of being so afraid of vomiting that he panicked every time he had indigestion, and would ask for reassurance when he got biro ink on his hands; a nurse practitioner told me off for calling this a 'phobia'. Naming is power, and that power was not mine to appropriate.

When I went through the published paper, it was no surprise to read that 'Autistic mothers reported significantly more difficulty than non-autistic mothers in being able to communicate effectively with professionals about their child and experienced a greater amount of anxiety when needing to react with professionals. Forty-four per cent of autistic mothers reported that this caused them to experience difficulties with communication.' They were also 'more likely to feel misunderstood by professionals and to end up in conflict over their child with professionals' and 'struggled more than non-autistic mothers to know which personal details are the most appropriate to share with professionals'.[130] I highlighted that last bit: whether I'm seeing a health professional on my own behalf or as my son's mother, my instinct is to present them with every detail that is, or might be relevant. I've learned to curb this to some extent, as the professionals so obviously find it unhelpful and annoying.

Recently I came across an example of this in a different medical context. It appeared in a letter to the editor of the *Inflammatory Bowel Diseases* journal, written in response to a paper on the relatively high prevalence of IBDs in children with autism. The authors of the letter present the case of a twenty-seven-year-old man who had been diagnosed with Asperger's Syndrome at thirteen, and presented with bowel symptoms. In their words, 'He was talking all the time during consultation visit, trying to disorientate the physician from his diagnostic approach. He assumed an association of diarrhea with a "nonhealthy" diet he was following, and he invented different "pathophysiological" scenarios for his symptoms.' They go on to suggest that '[t]his case highlights the impact of a personality with ASD on early diagnosis of IBD' and conclude that 'patients with ASD presenting with subtle IBD-related symptoms represent a challenging clinical scenario, heralding an increased vigilance from consulting physicians'.[131]

I don't suppose for a moment that the young man in this case study meant to be obstructive, or was trying to 'disorientate' the physician on purpose, but you don't need to read between the lines to realize that the physician found him strange, and very

annoying with it. Asperger didn't take to you; Kanner seems to
have despised the mothers of his patients. If you were anything
like me, you would have picked up on Asperger's irritation; this,
amplified by your memories of tense professional encounters from
your past, would have made you nervous; the more nervous you
became, the more you would have talked. It's no wonder that
60 per cent of the autistic mothers surveyed for the recent study
'reported experiencing such high levels of anxiety that they could
not think clearly'.[132]

If you irritate someone by talking too much at a party, you feel
it – the shame, the sense of social failure, all of that – but the real
consequences are trivial. If you irritate someone by talking too
much in a consulting room, the consequences can be serious. And
not just for you. I'm not saying that doctors or nurses or psychologists punish people deliberately, but they are human beings
acting in relationship to other human beings, and relationships
will always exercise a gravitational pull on human judgement.

As you might expect of such a powerful monster – mother of
monsters, no less – the Refrigerator Mother escaped the confines
of clinical discourse and started raging about the newspapers
and the radio and the bookshops, horrifying the general public
(and fascinating them too). She was the perfect monster for her
time and place, the post-war America Betty Friedan critiqued in
The Feminine Mystique, where women were expected not only
to return to their homes, but in in some metonymic way *become*
them; the consumer paradise of post-war America, where every
mother and homemaker could aspire to own a refrigerator. A successful psychological freak needs a showman as well as a stage: the
nineteenth-century French Hysteric had Jean-Martin Charcot;
the Refrigerator Mother had Bruno Bettelheim. Charcot exhibited

his patients directly in person, at public lectures; Bettelheim used the written word.

Bettelheim's book *The Empty Fortress: Infantile Autism and the Birth of the Self* came out in 1967 and was a best-seller. It tells a compelling story of a hero (Bettelheim) rescuing helpless, innocent children (his autistic patients) from cold, death-dealing, unnatural women (their mothers). As well as the authority deriving from his clinical experience (which some have questioned),[133] Bettelheim draws on the authority of his lived experience as a survivor of ten months in Nazi concentration camps. In the introduction to the book, he describes a horrifying withdrawal from self that he observed in some of his fellow inmates: 'In the German concentration camps I witnessed with utter disbelief the nonreacting of certain prisoners to their most cruel experience.' These prisoners, Bettelheim writes, have found a way to blot out the pain and fear of their situation, but at a terrible cost: such a prisoner 'who let the SS get hold of him, not just physically but emotionally too, went on to internalize the SS attitude that he was less than a man, that he was not to act on his own, that he had no personal will'.[134] Once he has 'transformed his inner experience to accord with his outer reality'[135] in this way, the prisoner will have 'lost' his 'humanity'.[136]

It was inevitable that these experiences would leave Bettelheim with an overwhelming amount of trauma to work through. Initially, he attempted to do this through his academic writing. In 1943, four years after arriving in the States, Bettelheim published a paper entitled 'Individual and mass behaviour in extreme situations', in which he suggested that the broken prisoners he had observed in the camp had been 'effectively turned into children'.[137] The paper was a great success, and prompted the University of Chicago to invite Bettelheim to take over its 'Orthogenic' school

for disturbed children. Bettelheim, his analogy between prisoner and child still fresh in his mind, thought he perceived a
particularly strong similarity between the demeanour of the hol-
lowed-out prisoner and that of the autistic child, and this drove
him to the conclusion that they must arise from a like – or at least
analogous – cause:

> Some victims of the concentration camps had lost their
> humanity in response to extreme situations. Autistic chil-
> dren withdraw from the world before their humanity ever
> really develops. Could there be any connection, I won-
> dered, between the impact of the two kinds of humanity I
> had known – one inflicted for political reasons on victims
> of a social system, the other perhaps a self-chosen state of
> dehumanization (if one may speak of choice in an infant's
> responses)?[138]

According to Bettelheim, childhood autism (which, as historian Adam Feinstein points out, was still largely confused with
childhood schizophrenia) was entirely a response to pathological
parenting. He wrote that 'I believe the initial cause of [the autistic
child's] withdrawal is... the child's correct interpretation of the
negative emotions with which the most significant figures in his
environment approach him.'[139] The autism then develops through
a vicious cycle of mutual miscommunication between mother
and child:

> The infant, because of pain or discomfort and the anxiety
> they cause, or because he misreads the mother's actions
> or feelings, or correctly assesses her negative feelings, may
> retreat from her and the world. The mother, for her part,

either frustrated in her motherly feelings, or out of her own anxiety, may respond not with gentle pursuit, but with anger or injured indifference.[140]

What frightens me so much when I read *The Empty Fortress* from a mother's perspective, as so many mothers in the late sixties must have done, is how subtle these manifestations of damaging motherhood can be. Bettelheim is not talking about a baby who is physically abused or neglected, or shouted at, or left alone to cry for hours; the failures he observes are much, much slighter than that. When the infant is nursed, for example, it matters whether he is held 'gently or rigidly', 'securely or anxiously'; 'whether he is carefully "heard," or emotionally ignored'. While it is true that 'the infant can make it clear, through the way he holds his body, whether or not he feels comfortably held, he cannot ensure that this active expression of his feelings will meet with a positive response. That will depend on how the mother reacts.'[141]

As time goes on, according to Bettelheim, the infant's success or failure in producing the correct maternal reactions will shape the infant's 'view of himself and the world'. In terms which recall Winnicott's facilitating environment and Bion's alpha-function, Bettelheim asserts that 'Typically for the human infant, relating and communicating have their roots in his cooing or crying, and the mother's appropriate and positive response. As she helps him sort out pain from hunger through her different responses, and as different ministrations relieve different forms of discomfort, the infant learns to distinguish between his own feelings of discomfort.' In this way 'the feeling of self (or the body ego) begins to develop'.[142] Before birth, the mother is the physical environment in which the foetus grows; after birth, she is the emotional environment in which the mind grows. God forbid she should be the wrong sort of psychological soil.

I hadn't read *The Empty Fortress* when I had my child, but I had been impressed by a documentary on Bettelheim's work 'rescuing children from psychosis' (his words), and you know about the Winnicott and the Bion. I've told you how anxious I was before I'd even entered motherhood, how determined I was to put myself to one side and transform myself from a faulty person into a perfect location. So you can imagine how I felt when I realized that my baby's father was better at recognizing his different cries than I was.

Bettelheim was one of the all-time great mum-shamers. Feinstein quotes autism professionals who had 'heard that Bettelheim often pointed to a large, abstract stone statue representing a mother and told the children: "This is what your mother is like: cold and hard."'[143] It was only after his death that the stories of his own cruelty to the children in his care emerged. This behaviour, his own traumatic history and the manner of his death – suicide by suffocation – all suggest to me that his persistent shaming of mothers was his way of trying to expel his own violent feelings of shame into someone else. It is a mother's job to carry other people's shame, just as it is her job to carry the unacknowledged truth of human dependency. The two are linked: vulnerability and dependency, in a culture organized around the ideal of the independent self, are felt to be shameful conditions.

It feels especially shameful when you are supposed to be taking the caring role. Shameful, and also dangerous for the person you are caring for. I understood that one of my most important functions as a mother was to make my child feel safe, but I didn't know how I was going to manage to pull off what I could only see as a flagrant con trick. If there was one thing I knew – and still know – it's that the world is *not* safe. If it was safe, then why was it constantly printing and broadcasting so much evidence that it wasn't? All the stories of accidentally crushed babies or suffocated babies or choked babies or overheated babies or babies put down to sleep in the wrong way so that they died in the night, babies in the wrong position in buggies, babies in incorrectly placed car seats, babies with meningitis that no one spotted till it was too late... To which my obsessive compulsive imagination added: babies dropped onto hard floors, babies stabbed with knives in kitchen accidents, babies accidentally wounded because they had been winded too hard, babies falling under cars, babies falling under buses, babies hit by trains, babies dropped in a crowd and stamped to death. Worse than that were the mental pictures of me harming my child – throwing him under the car, giving in to an impulse to knife him in the kitchen, and others I can't bring myself to set down even sixteen-odd years later, even now... I was too frightened to tell my GP or health visitor about these last pictures until I came across a description of post-natal OCD in a book and realized what they were. I still wasn't convinced that the world wasn't dangerous to my son, but at least I finally understood that *I* wasn't – not physically, anyway.

It was a relief to tick 'potentially murderous' off my long list of motherly shortcomings. It was quite long enough as it was. I've mentioned that I was not as good at distinguishing my son's different cries as my husband was; even though this became relatively unimportant quite quickly, as our son developed other ways of communicating, I feel the shame of it to this day, of not living up to the ideal of the naturally intuitive mother, and having a husband who seemed closer to her than I was. It was not something I could ever have admitted at the time.

The more practical aspects of motherhood – what the feminist philosopher Sara Ruddick terms 'preservative love'[144] – were also problematic for me. Although I wanted to have my baby close to me, I was also anxious about handling him; I am poorly coordinated, and I knew it, and I was afraid that my clumsiness might hurt the baby, so I passed on as much of the practical care to my poor husband (who was working full-time) as I could. The breastfeeding didn't work. I had my mother constantly coming up from London to help me, and when she went away on holiday just after my thyroid diagnosis, I broke down and that's when we hired the nanny. She would arrive in the morning with her eighteen-month-old daughter and they would take the baby out for the day; he took to them and they took to him; she could drive and take him to places, expanding his world in a way that I couldn't. She was only meant to cover a couple of weeks, but the arrangement worked so well – for her, for me and for the baby – and I was still as ill after two weeks, so she stayed, part-time, coming in for a whole year. Sometimes we went out, the four of us together, to soft play or to toddler music groups, and we all got along and it was fine.

At the same time, I felt terrible, because I couldn't do it all by myself, because I was getting support by exploiting another mother's maternal labour, because we could afford to pay someone to support me when so many families couldn't, but also because we couldn't really afford it – my deficiencies were straining the household budget and I wasn't bringing in any money myself. That I managed to look after my son by myself for days at a time didn't do much to reassure me: when he was in my care I was scared most of the time in an all-pervasive, bone-saturating way that I just wasn't when he was being cared for by someone else. He deserved so much better than me. If I occasionally heard him call his justly loved nanny 'Mummy', that was all the punishment I deserved.

Except he wasn't punishing me. He didn't call his nanny 'Mummy' because he was rejecting me or even because he was confused, but because he wanted her attention and couldn't say her name. He knew I was his mother and he didn't seem to mind. Once I'd accepted that the breastfeeding wasn't happening, my son and I got on very well. We exchanged lots of smiles; we had conversations – wordless still, on his side, but conversations nonetheless. I made him laugh. He made me laugh. I read to him. I played with him. When he was upset, I held him. When he was tired, I rocked him to sleep. I was as far from being Bettelheim's stone statue as could be imagined. If anything, I was too pervious to my son's moods: when he was upset, I found it hard to stop myself getting upset too. If he was frantic, I could also become frantic. As he got older, that sometimes made it difficult to set down boundaries: my health visitor had to convince me that it was time to stop rocking him to sleep, and to let him begin to learn to soothe himself. When, at two years old, he went through a phase of crying inconsolably every time I dropped him off at nursery, I phoned the same health visitor for advice, and she told me, firmly, that no, I should not give up and take him out of day-care: 'He can't be allowed to make big decisions for himself,' she said. 'It can't be up to him. That's your job.'

Yesterday evening, after I'd finished writing the last paragraph, I went downstairs and talked to my husband about those fraught early years. I said I'd realized that the only person who'd thought I was a bad mother was me. He hadn't; the nanny hadn't; the day-care staff who took over from her hadn't; the GP hadn't; the health visitor hadn't; my own mother hadn't (although she thought I wasn't firm enough with my son – there's always something). Neither the Home Start volunteer nor the MIND volunteer who supported me while I learned to take him out into the frightening world thought I was a bad mother. The psychologist who asked me to rate my anxiety as a percentage while I moved nearer to the riverbank with my son didn't think I was either. But I was ashamed, and I was ashamed because I needed all these people to help me mother my son. I knew plenty of mothers whose parents lived too far away to help them, who hadn't used any form of childcare for the first year. I knew – and this was a particular sticking point – an awful lot of women whose husbands left almost all the childcare, and the cooking, and the housework, to their wives. Complaining about menfolk is a big part of early-motherhood socializing, and I couldn't join in (neither, to be fair, could the stay-at-home dad who was a central member of my coffee-morning group). If another mother told me that I was lucky, and that my husband was 'wonderful', I would hear it as a judgement, as if I'd got away with something I shouldn't have.

In a culture that defines an adult to be an independent individual, and a family as an independent household consisting of two parents and their offspring, a mother's own dependence on others to help her do her job is one of those forms of dependency that is supposed to remain invisible: a carer shouldn't need care, and any visible need means that their fitness to care for others can be called into question. Over the last few years, I have been following Icelandic politician and disability activist Freyja Haraldsdóttir on social media, where she has been recording her legal battle to be allowed to be considered as a foster carer. Haraldsdóttir was born with osteogenesis imperfecta. She lives and works with the support of personal assistants, and uses a wheelchair. Her support needs have not prevented her from gaining a degree, working, advocating for other disabled people, travelling (when I first came across her we were both attending a Disability Studies conference in the UK) or serving as a member of the Icelandic parliament. In this respect, she is part of that sub-set of visibly disabled people who are officially recognized as efficacious and successful in the public realm, and acknowledged as contributing to the public good. Disability activists in the Global North have spent decades fighting for the right for disabled people to access education and employment; in many countries, this right is enshrined in law. The implementation of disability legislation might be patchy, to put it mildly, but it is there.

In her book *Female Forms: Experiencing and Understanding Disability*, published twenty years ago, Carol Thomas argued that discussions around definitions of disability and disability rights had tended to be 'male-focused', with an emphasis on employment-related injuries and on the need for help to find and maintain employment.[145] However, as she points out, where women are concerned, barriers to reproduction rather than production have often been more important. While disability activism has neglected reproductive rights in favour of rights to employment, mainstream feminism – able-bodied, white and middle-class – has been more concerned with establishing women's rights *not* to reproduce, *not* to take a caring role and *not* to have to define themselves relationally. This is all very necessary, but it is also worth remembering that, on the whole, it is not able-bodied, white, middle-class women whose fertility is seen as something that needs to be contained, or who have been subjected to forced contraception, abortion, sterilization or adoption. There are some contentious areas, such as pre-natal genetic screening for conditions such as Down's Syndrome, where the history of women's oppression through forced reproduction and caring tangles painfully with the continued struggle of disabled people to establish the right to exist and live at all. A disabled woman may have succeeded in staying alive, growing up, receiving an education, living independently from her family and working, but when it comes to her attempts to enter into the relationships which are seen as part of adulthood – sexual relationships, the caring relationship with a child – she may find herself walking or wheeling into a brick wall.

It took Haraldsdóttir five years to win the right to be assessed as a potential foster parent. The initial ruling against her was made partly on the grounds that there was no research available on foster parenting in households where the parent relied on personal assistance. How, the agency argued, could they know that it would work? One might just as reasonably ask: how could they know that it wouldn't? Given how much parents vary, and children vary, and situations vary, I would argue that every time a particular adult sets out to parent a particular child, they are embarking on an unrepeatable experiment.

In many respects, Melanie Mahjenta's story – like yours, and the stories of the Kanner mothers – will be familiar to any mother of an autistic child, whether she herself is autistic or not. There is the realization, at some point, that her child is not developing in the same way as most other children their age; the disapproving looks and comments from family, other parents, and strangers, and their suspicion that her mothering must have something to do with the child's 'bad' behaviour/late potty training/feeding prob-lems/social withdrawal; the painful sight of their child's being rejected by their peers; the struggle – the never-ending struggle – to get that child the support they need.

My mother told me that the staff at my nursery school thought I needed to be checked out: sometimes I would ball my fists and grit my teeth – I was 'stimming', in other words. She told me about the paediatrician who snapped at her to control me when I had a meltdown during an examination. She told me about the teachers in primary school who didn't believe that I could read as well as she said I could. And I remember the difficulties with other children, the stammering, the ostracism, the bullying, the educational psychologist, the headmaster's refusal to listen to her. I remember how gladly she seized on my above-average IQ as an explanation for my problems – what mother wouldn't? When I think about how much it cost them to send me to a school outside the state system – and my brother too, because they had to be fair – I feel both grateful and guilty. When I remember how many times she had to apologize to people after I'd made some interesting observation aloud, I feel embarrassed for her. And, now that I'm a mother myself, when I think of how she had to witness the unhappiness, the depression, the anxiety of my later girlhood and early adulthood, and how I took out my helpless anger on her, I wish she were still here now, so that I could say that I finally understand, and that I appreciate how hard she must have had to fight for me. She didn't realize that she was the mother of an autistic child – in those days, nobody did.

I sometimes wonder what difference it would have made if she had known. Would she have been resistant, at least at first, bridling at the idea that something could be 'wrong' with her child? Would she have spent more time in my primary school headmaster's office, arguing for the support she knew I needed? Would she have managed to obtain further support for me in secondary school, so that I could remain in the state system? When I reached adulthood, would she have been too frightened for me to let me leave home, if I had wanted to? Would she have sought out the support of other mothers, and given support back? Knowing my mother, she would have swapped – or augmented – her Jewish voluntary committees for autism-related ones. She would have got involved with the National Autistic Society. If she had discovered that there was no specifically Jewish organization to help autistic people and their families, she would have helped found it. I can easily imagine her as one of those passionate and determined autism activist mothers, who, in most countries at least, were able to overwrite the Refrigerator Mother narrative with a more positive one of their own. The text that marked the beginning of this narrative shift was a book by a father of an autistic child, the research psychologist Bernard Rimland, which was published in 1964. In *Infantile Autism: The Syndrome and Its Implications for a Neural Theory of Behavior*, he set out the argument that autism was not psychogenic but biological.[146] Research by another psychologist, Eric Schopler, confirmed this view, indicating that the parental behaviour which Kanner, Bettelheim and the rest had been observing was not the cause of autism in their children, but a reaction to it. Parents, he argued, should be seen as allies, as co-therapists working with professionals in the best interests of the autistic child.

Maggi Golding provides a brief account of Rimland and Schopler's crucial interventions in her introduction to a collection of autobiographical pieces by the mothers of autistic children, *Autism Mothers Speak Out: Stories of Advocacy and Activism from Around the World*.[147] As the pieces in the book testify, mothering an autistic child is an overwhelming business, involving work on many fronts; it can easily take over a woman's life. To call oneself an 'autism mother' or 'autism mom' is to fashion oneself a positive identity from this struggle, while expressing solidarity and commonality with other mothers in the same situation. There are T-shirts you can buy, featuring statements such as 'Proud Autism Mom', 'It Takes A Special Mom To Hear What A Child Cannot Say', and 'God Found Some Of The Strongest Women And Unleashed Them To Be Autism Moms'. The wording of some of these T-shirts refers directly to the social burden their wearers carry, and indicates the kind of encounters that a mother would need to arm herself to face: 'I Am The Proud Parent Of A Child With Autism I Have More To Worry About Than Your Opinion Don't Judge What You Don't Know'. Much as you did, mothers of autistic children still face stigma by association, even if they are no longer refrigerated.

A number of writers, such as Adam Feinstein, Steve Silberman and Jordynn Jack,[148] have traced this shift in the cultural history of autism in more detail, as has Amy C. Sousa in her paper 'From Refrigerator Mothers to Warrior-Heroes: The Cultural Identity Transformation of Mothers Raising Children with Intellectual Disabilities'.[149] I am sure that you would rather be a hero than a faulty domestic appliance, but, as Sousa points out, the effect of this shift from one cultural archetype to another has not been to lift the burden mothers carry, but to transform it into something else. The 'warrior-hero' archetype 'places a cultural expectation on mothers to do battle to attain resources and possible cures for their children, ultimately shifting the historical burden on mothers from causing the intellectual disabilities of their children to curing them'.[150] It would not be enough, now, for you to take Franz to Asperger's clinic, and accept, passively, whatever treatment was offered. You would be judged if you failed to take a pro-active role – but you would be judged in any case. Passive mothers do not care enough; pro-active ones are difficult and aggressive. Melanie Mahjenta's story was certainly complicated by her own autism, but non-autistic mothers of autistic children would recognize the resistance and hostility she faced as she tried to get the right diagnosis and support for her daughter.

In a recent paper published in *Disability & Society*, Katherine Runswick-Cole and Sara Ryan, both non-autistic mothers of autistic children, address the impossible situation of battling autism mothers. While they will find themselves 'held responsible for their child's genetic inheritance and for fixing their children's impaired bodies and minds', many will come to realize that 'it is not their children who need fixing but the world around them'.[151] They will then take on the burden that Sousa identified, 'as they (are forced to) campaign for both the recognition of the value and humanity of their children, and others'. What they cannot realize, at first, is that they are fated to become part of a 'cycle of failure', in which successive generations of parents duplicate the efforts of their predecessors as they seek to 'raise awareness', hoping that by drawing public and political attention to the situation of their children, they will be able to effect significant and lasting change.

Runswick-Cole and Ryan set out the reasons why, despite generations of struggle, this change refuses to happen: as disabled children grow up, their parents' focus shifts from provision for children to provision for adults, and they move into a different sphere of activism. At the same time, lack of communication and cooperation between different generations of parents means that each new generation of mother-activists will repeat the labours of the generation before, unaware that they are not, after all, venturing into pioneer territory. They are led to believe, not least by the charities for which they are such valuable fundraisers, that the reality of their lives and that of their children is 'hidden', and that the public and policy-makers, once made aware of these hidden truths, will feel compelled to do the necessary work. Unfortunately, as Runswick-Cole and Ryan point out, this is an illusion:

> The harsh truth that both parents and the big charities seem reluctant to face is that successive British governments have known about the social injustices in the lives of disabled children and families and have done little to bring about change... Disabled children and adults continue to occupy the position of wasted humans (Bauman 2004) alongside others minoritised through the workings of race, class, (hetero)sexuality, religion, colonialism, poverty and gender.[152]

When a campaign focuses on the stories of individual disabled people, their mothers and their families, it allows these 'workings' and their role in the struggles of disabled people and their families to remain unexamined, and the systems which rely on them to remain unchallenged. The threats for you and for Fritz were stark and clear: fascist states do not attempt to hide or soften their agendas where mothers or disabled people are concerned, and nor do they tolerate protest. In early twenty-first-century Britain, the forces behind social injustices are not always immediately perceptible – you need the right conceptual tools to help you see them. One concept central to Ryan and Runswick-Cole's analysis is 'neoliberalism'. As the books and articles I've been reading tend to assume familiarity with the idea, I've had to look online for a decent basic definition. Here's one from Kean Birch on theconversation.com, a website where academics write for general readers:

Neoliberalism is regularly used in popular debate around the world to define the last 40 years. It's used to refer to an economic system in which the 'free' market is extended to every part of our public and personal worlds. The transformation of the state from a provider of public welfare to a promoter of markets and competition helps to enable this shift.[153]

When we consider the effects of neoliberalism on the lives of mothers of autistic children, the particularly salient features are the extension of the free market to 'every part' of our 'personal worlds' and the 'transformation of the state from a provider of public welfare to a promoter of markets and competition'. Neoliberalism means austerity, which means fewer public resources for disabled people; it means a move from welfare to 'workfare',[154] in which state benefits are awarded not simply on the basis of need, but on the understanding that the recipients must actively seek work and take any that they are offered; it means that disabled people and their families are positioned as 'consumers' of state and voluntary services, who must bear the burden first of making an informed choice, and then of competing for the scarce funds required to realize that choice. This burden will be heavier and more complex if the mother is disabled herself, from an ethnic minority, economically or educationally disadvantaged, single, already reliant on benefits, or cannot afford to take the time out of paid employment required to be an effective Autism Mother. It doesn't help that employment for many mothers is precarious and low-paid. At the same time, contemporary 'ideological constructions of intensive mothering'[155] which demand that a mother take responsibility for every aspect of her child's development, under the guidance of the appropriate professionals, set women up to fail. Even with every advantage, it is harder than ever for a mother to be 'good enough'; for the mother of a child whose development is judged to deviate from the norm, it is well-nigh impossible.

A family which requires extra support to raise children is a burden on the state, a 'problem family', a 'troubled family', a suspected nest of scroungers. A good neoliberal citizen is a resilient, entrepreneurial, flexible, productive, independent, earning-and-spending sort of citizen; a good neoliberal mother is the mother who raises that citizen while being such a citizen herself.

A good neoliberal Autism Mother willingly takes on the burden of ensuring her child's well-being, which she does in a resilient, independent and entrepreneurial fashion: fundraising, buying goods and services for her child, possibly establishing services for her child and other children like them, exhibiting both determination and positivity as she goes. When services fail or are abusive, it is often the parents who end up functioning as unpaid quality control officers for institutions which cannot or will not adequately regulate themselves. We are so used to consuming human-interest stories in which parents raise the alarm that it is easy to forget that THEY SHOULD NOT HAVE TO DO IT.

When it comes to holding failing services to account, Ryan herself has more experience than anyone should ever have. In July 2013, her eighteen-year-old autistic son, Connor Sparrowhawk, who had learning disabilities and epilepsy, drowned in his bath at a National Health Service Assessment and Treatment Unit (ATU). He was known to have seizures, but no risk assessment had been carried out before he had been left in the bathroom alone. The NHS Trust claimed Connor died of natural causes, but Ryan knew that his death was preventable, the consequence of neglect, and she called for an independent investigation. After five years of struggle, during which Ryan was subject to continual mother-blaming – the Southern Health Trust waited only one day after Connor's death to circulate a memo about a blog she had written – and had received anonymous abuse from one of its employees, the Trust was found liable for the preventable deaths of Connor and another patient, and fined £2 million.

That Ryan was able to prevail against all the forces of institutional inertia, self-protectiveness and downright abuse to get the judgement her son deserved was not only down to her own resourcefulness, but also to a campaign of collective action. Prior to his death, Connor had become familiar to Ryan's readers as 'Laughing Boy' or 'LB', a character in Ryan's light-hearted blog about her family, mydaftlife.wordpress.com. In 2013, after Connor was admitted to the ATU, the blog changed, 'bec[oming] a grim diary of the 107 days he spent in the unit before his death'.[156] Taking Connor's pseudonym as a starting point, Ryan's family, friends and followers set out to counter the Trust's efforts to exonerate themselves and blame Ryan by rallying around the Twitter hashtag #JusticeforLB. As Ryan and Runswick-Cole explain, 'the responsibility for gaining answers and accountability became a collective endeavour among a diverse range of people, the majority of whom had never met Connor or his family'.[157] In 2014, the anniversary of those 107 days was marked by a coordinated international effort to fundraise for legal fees and raise awareness of the lives of people with learning disabilities. Campaigners 'adopted' days, 'to take part in sporting events in Connor's memory, to create artwork, hold cake sales, produce films and animations, and perform musical events; there were academic talks, workshops, the creation of a #JusticeforLB quilt, bus rides and so much more'.[158] I was one of many thousands of people who found out about Connor's story, and the campaign, through the use of this memorable and powerful hashtag.

Runswick-Cole and Ryan describe this collective action as an example of 'unmothering' – and propose it as a more effective alternative to traditional mother-advocacy. The concept of unmothering 'seeks to disrupt the idea that the mother alone is responsible for raising children. Unmothering appeals to collectivity and the interdependence of the disability commons, challenging the discourse of individualisation and responsibilisation of the family that permeates current English government policy rhetoric'.[159] The concept of unmothering appeals very much to me, as does the concept of the 'disability commons', which is a term for what happens when disabled people, their families and others come together to 'refuse' disabled people's 'constitution as "wasted humans"' through acts of shared resistance, advocacy and support.[160] To me, these ideas offer liberation from the narrow silos of interest and experience which keep individual families apart from each other, generations separated, and disabled people and the mothers of disabled people at loggerheads.

All too often, I see the most bitter conflicts arising, both online and off, between some parents of autistic children with high support needs and some self-advocating autistic adults. To some parents, any positive assertion of autistic identity threatens their attempts to secure support for their child, which they understand to depend upon the fullest acknowledgement of the difficulties they and their child face as a result of that child's autism; to some autistic adults, any narrative which foregrounds these difficulties represents an attempt to downgrade their humanity – *our* humanity, I should say.

I like to think, perhaps naively, that in desiring the best and fullest possible lives for autistic people and their families, regardless of the level of support required, we really ought to be fighting on the same side. Any mother of any child has the potential to be both an oppressor and an ally. At the same time, every mother is also a person and no person should face sanctions simply for expressing her own feelings about her own experience of mothering (just as I'm doing here). I would just suggest that if you wouldn't want someone to post footage of your worst moments on the internet, or discuss your incontinence on a public forum without granting you any anonymity, or appear in campaign videos in which they speak about their fantasies of killing you while you sit next to them, you might perhaps think twice before doing any of these things to your child. When you are sharing space with someone, it is never all right to talk about them as if they were not there.

And I say that even though I've done it myself, sometimes – to my own child, to other people's children. It's one of those casually dehumanizing habits we can fall into without thinking. I'd like to think that such small lapses are forgivable. Most shortcomings are. To come up short in some way, to be insufficient in ourselves, to rely on others to look after ourselves, and, in some ways, to *be* ourselves at all, seems to me to be as good a definition of human as any other. It's a definition that relies not on our abilities or capacities but on our mutual dependence: I need, therefore I am. It is a definition informed by the Ethics of Care developed by Virginia Held,[161] Eva Feder Kittay and others, which centres the relationship of the carer and the cared-for, in place of the contractual relationships between equals which lie at the centre of traditional morality. It is informed also by the idea of the dis/human, which was formulated by Dan Goodley and Runswick-Cole as a recognition of the ways in which people with profound intellectual disabilities can offer 'new ways of thinking about our humanness in relation to interdependence, mutuality and interconnection'.[162]

Interdependence, mutuality, interconnection. We can use these terms to think about how we are as human mothers, and as the mothers of humans. How we need each other's help to be good enough. How Winnicott, who came up with the concept of the good-enough mother, did actually recognize that his good-enough mother was, among other things, a mother who was adequately supported. How there really never was any shame in either of us needing help and having to look to others for solutions to our mothering problems. How there was never really any contradiction between being mothers and being human beings with our own needs and dependencies. No two mothers are alike, but no one can mother alone. This notion, that the mother–baby dyad, standing apart from all others, is an ideal template for child-rearing, is a collective delusion quite specific to our culture in the Global North, and it would be better for everyone if we collectively snapped out of it.[163]

You needed more support than usual. I did too. What neither of us ever needed was absolution.

From your Weird Sister Mother,

Joanne

Katharina Kepler

Katharina Kepler (née Guldenmann) was born somewhere between 1547 and 1550 in the village of Eltingen, in the German principality of Württemberg. Her parents ran an inn, and her father served as mayor for some eighteen years. Katharina did not go to school, and would have helped her parents to maintain their household, their inn, their animals and their crops until she married Heinrich Kepler, a merchant's son, in her early twenties. In December 1571, she gave birth to her first child, named Johannes. In 1575, the growing family moved to Leonberg, which Katharina would consider home for the rest of her life. Katharina's life was far from easy: her husband had a habit of abandoning the family periodically; he often left Katharina to cope on her own, and died in 1590. Her second son, also called Heinrich, grew up to be like his father, incapable of settling. Fortunately, her eldest son Johannes did well for himself, going to university at Tübingen and eventually rising to be imperial mathematician to Rudolph II, the Holy Roman Emperor. Johannes was not one to abandon his family: he did his best to help Heinrich, and when Katharina was accused of witchcraft in 1615, he travelled back to Württemberg to help her, eventually defending her in her trial five years later. He was successful, though Katharina did not live long after her acquittal, and was never able to return to her house in Leonberg. She has a presence there now, in the form of a statue. Using the surviving court records, including Johannes's detailed evidence and arguments, the historian Ulinka Rublack has been able to construct an account of the life of this ordinary, illiterate woman, and when I read Rublack's book *The Astronomer and the Witch: Johannes Kepler's Fight for His Mother*, I knew that I wanted to write to Katharina.[164]

Letter to Katharina Kepler

Dear Katharina

I hope that whoever reads this aloud to you does so patiently, and with good grace. You can hardly be blamed for the fact that no one in your birthplace in late sixteenth-century Württemberg thought it necessary to teach you to read. Nor is it your fault that your son Johannes's success as an imperial mathematician has taken him so far away that he cannot communicate with you except by letter. Nor is it your fault that your husband left you a widow some years ago, and there is no man in your house to read you this letter, which means that you have had to ask a favour of a male neighbour. As a widow of some years' standing, you have had to ask a lot of favours – there are many limits to what a woman is allowed to do for herself, legally speaking, in the town of Leonberg, in the Duchy of Württemberg, in the early 1600s. As Johannes will point out to the court when he comes to defend you, you could hardly request these favours without asserting yourself, and it is hardly your fault that such assertion is seen as unwomanly, and therefore suspect. It creates bad feeling when an old woman importunes her neighbours, but an old woman still has to survive.

I hope whoever reads this letter is kinder than Johannes's old schoolfriend, the town schoolmaster, who testified that you had made a nuisance of yourself pestering him to read out your son's letters from Prague; as if this were not persecution enough, he claimed that you had then used magic to appear through a closed door in his house and insist that he write back to Johannes for you. Apparently, even your gratitude and generosity were supernaturally destructive. He alleged that you stopped him on his way to church, begging, 'You have done so much for me, and I have a very good wine in my cellar. Do come and have some.'[165] He claimed that the pain in his legs began after only one sip. Soon, he needed two sticks to walk. Not long after that, he was paralysed. It was all your witchcraft, he said.

So I hope you've asked someone else this time.

When I first thought of writing to some of my weird sisters from history, witches were among the first women who came to mind (I first heard that phrase, 'weird sisters', as a collective term for the witches in *Macbeth*, with their potions and prophecies). And not just to my mind: I would tell people that I wanted to write about autistic women from history (by which I mean weird women, women who did not behave as they should, and not because they would not, but because they *could* not) and a common response was: 'Right, like witches?' So naturally I began to read about witches. I expected to find village outsiders, the obviously, point-at-her-in-the-street weird women without the usual connections or kin, women without property, irreligious women. I also had in mind the feminist re-visioning of witches as wise, healing women whose powers presented a direct challenge to the patriarchy.

Of course, I was wrong on both counts. It turned out that, in the late sixteenth and early seventeenth centuries, when accusations of witchcraft were at their height in Europe, *anyone* could be accused, whether male or female, older or younger, powerful or powerless, rich or poor.[166] Witchcraft was bound up with heresy, and anyone could be a heretic. It was also a convenient explanation of any misfortune, large or small, at a time when few other explanations were available. And misfortunes were constant: people sickened and died, the animals on which they depended for subsistence sickened and died, accidents befell people and animals alike, crops were blighted, scarce possessions broke or burned or went missing. In the small, tight-knit community where you lived, there seems to have been a fairly steady low level of suspicion circulating; people kept notes on each other. The standards of proof for an accusation of witchcraft were intended to be stringent, but the nature of that proof was slippery and debatable. And, then, as now, suspicion was contagious. This was crucial in your case, as the law held that if a person was widely held to be a witch, then this was itself a reason to think the accusations were true.

Once the level of suspicion and number of accusations against you had reached a critical point, your arrest and trial became inevitable. Every little gesture or speech of yours, every act of kindness and mutual aid, every request for like help from others, every one of the many small acts which made up the usual currency of your life as a townswoman, was picked up and examined and found to be suspect. Although there was little privacy in your community, your habit of entering other people's houses was suddenly sinister. Your requests for favours were particularly out of the way and unreasonable. People remembered times when you had spoken harshly to them or brushed up against them in the street and realized belatedly that their illnesses had begun at that very moment. If their animals had become ill, it was because you had touched or even just admired them. The cups of wine and herbal drinks you had poured for your neighbours were revealed to be potions saturated with magical harm. A healing prayer you had shared became a demonic spell.

I don't know what would have happened to you if it had not been for your extraordinary eldest son. When Johannes took on the task of defending you, he brought to it all his considerable resources of intellect, education, experience and scholarly status. He applied the same scientific rigour he brought to his writings on nature and astronomy to the evidence offered against you, taking up each accusation in turn and proposing an alternative, benign explanation. He drew the court's attention to the social double bind you were in as a widow of independent means, who had no choice but to assert herself in the course of her daily life, even when this behaviour provoked disapproval and censure. As he put it in one of his legal submissions:

> [Katharina] has had to defend herself among the common rabble during the twenty-eight years [of her widowhood], during which she has lived without help and as a widow with her many immature children, has scantily fed herself, improved her land, and defended her interests, and sometimes been drawn into various quarrels, unhappiness and enmity.[167]

It clearly didn't escape him that, although anyone and everyone might fall under suspicion of witchcraft, the few who were formally accused, tried and sometimes executed in Württemberg were almost invariably widows. He also speculated that – at least in your case – a disgust of the elderly female body might be another factor behind your prosecution. You were, after all, the oldest woman in Leonberg.

Johannes did not spare your feelings in his submissions to the court, about your appearance or anything else. Of course it was necessary, rhetorically speaking, to acknowledge the strength of his opponents' arguments before he set to undermine them, but it is not hard to see the very real filial irritation which animates his descriptions of your behaviour. He obviously knew you very well, loved you and took pains to understand you; at the same time, you obviously drove him to distraction. His occasional references to your 'imbecility', which make no obvious sense at all in the light of your ability to speak for yourself – you were able to satisfy your interrogators of your good knowledge of scripture and religion, for example – might perhaps make a little more sense as evidence of a son's frustration. Perhaps he'd explained something to you again and again and you'd forgotten; perhaps you'd persisted in behaviours which he'd advised against. Or perhaps he only threw the concept of 'imbecility' in as a way of drawing attention to your advanced age and frailty, as a way of suggesting that you could not be held legally responsible for your actions, and in the hope of arousing compassion.

You don't appear to have lacked capacity when it came to looking after your property and land, caring for animals, making up herbal remedies, running your household, religious observance, or any other area of practical knowledge. Throughout your life, you had proved yourself well able to look after yourself as well as others. When you were a younger woman, afflicted with a restless husband who kept abandoning his responsibilities to go off to war, you had on one occasion left your children with a friend and walked alone all the way from Württemberg to Flanders to persuade him to come home; you were successful, if only in the short term. You seem to have been in so many ways an admirable woman. What a pity it is that you never had the chance to become literate.

Despite your many capabilities and competences, there does appear to have been one area in which you stumbled fairly consistently, and this was in your relationships with others. You seem to have rubbed people up the wrong way, admittedly not a difficult thing to do in a close-knit, interdependent community, but Johannes's account of you suggests that you did it more than most. When it came to accusations of witchcraft, this was a fault that left you dangerously exposed. Women in early modern Lutheran Germany were seen as inherently 'heavily tainted by sin and characterized by their lack of reason'.[168] If a woman was to maintain any kind of good reputation, she could only do so through her consistent good behaviour: her neat and modest dress, her careful speech, her good housekeeping, her conspicuous Protestant busyness, her obvious care for others. She was to be subordinate and meek towards men, speak little, and when she did, speak gently.

You were not a gentle speaker. When you thought something needed saying, you said it. When you judged someone else to be in the wrong, you told them so. You would sometimes do so, as your son said, 'imprudently', without thinking through the consequences. When the matter of your status as a witch was in question, the 'quarrels, unhappiness and enmity' which had characterized some of your relationships with family and with neighbours would come back to haunt you.

One accusation, which must have been so hurtful, came from one of your own children. Heinrich was your second son. Shortly before Kepler senior abandoned his family for good, he had driven Heinrich out of the house. Left to his own devices, Heinrich had embarked on a rackety, unstable existence, not unlike that of the father who had at one point threatened to sell him. He was, variously, a soldier, a servant, a drummer and a beggar. Johannes did his best to help him, securing him a post as an imperial guardsman. Heinrich stayed in post for eight years, finally marrying and fathering two daughters. But in 1613, two years before you were accused, he was ill and poor and alone. He converted to Catholicism, and turned up at a monastery expecting care, only to be sent away. By 1615, he had left his daughters with Johannes and travelled to Leonberg, on the expectation that you would care for him instead.

From the moment Heinrich reappeared, he got you into trouble. He arrived on a cold weekend and demanded milk, when there was barely enough for you – at that time of year there was always barely enough of anything, as he should have known – so you had to ask the baker's wife to give you some. When the baker's wife said that she did not have enough and redirected you to another neighbour, you kept insisting, until the woman gave in. Then the baker's wife's calf fell ill. Gossiping with Ursula Reinbold, the woman who would become your principal accuser, she was led to wonder if perhaps you had been riding her calf until you wore it out, which was the sort of bad turn a witch might do for her neighbour. When this reached your ears, you chose to confront her, as was your way: "'Are you telling people that I have ridden your calf to death?' 'No,' the fifty-year-old baker's wife replied... 'but if I knew that you had done it, I would beat you down with a log.'"[169]

When the calf died, Heinrich, a dissatisfied son for whom your care could never be sufficiently tender, believed that you were the cause of it; he said so publicly, becoming the first to slander you as a witch. He died not long after, in February 1615, at his sister's house in Heumaden, but by then the damage was done. And all because he had turned up on your doorstep, demanding milk.

The breakdown of your relationship with Heinrich, painful though that must have been, was not the chief cause of your downfall. That was your dispute with Ursula Reinbold, the glazier's wife. In August 2015, Ursula and her brother were drinking with Lukas Einhorn, Leonberg's ducal governor and a friend of their family. As they talked, they complained to Einhorn about Ursula's recent lameness; they were certain, they said, that Katharina had bewitched her and made her ill. According to your biographer, Ulinka Rublack, one of them was heard to say that 'Nothing is to be gained by waiting around any longer,' after which Ursula added that 'That Kepler woman has to take her spell away before I die.'[170]

This put Einhorn under pressure. There were witchcraft trials under way in the nearby town of Sindelfingen, amid concern that witches might be causing real harm across the state of Württemberg. The Reinbolds were able to draw on a dense network of local connections: two of Ursula's brothers were employed by the Duke. In her distress and frustration at her unrelenting, worsening pain, Ursula continued to demand that her male relatives, and Einhorn, take urgent and forceful action on her behalf. In response, Einhorn dispensed with what should have been official procedure – noting the accusation, informing the local court and carrying out a formal interrogation – and, without any preliminaries, summoned you to come to his house and account for yourself.

When you arrived at the governor's house, Ursula and her brother were there to confront you. He shouted at you: you were a witch! You had given his sister a 'witches' brew'![171] He demanded that you work more magic and undo your spell. In your version of

the story, he then half-drew his sword. Your response was characteristic: you were shocked, but you managed to remain calm, and
you advocated for yourself as reasonably as you could. Rublack
sums up your arguments as follows:

> it was not legal and right to confront her with such allega-
> tions on her own. She was a very old woman and needed
> protection. How could she help Ursula if she had done
> nothing against her? God was the right doctor. This whole
> affair was of the devil. Next time there were any charges
> against her, she would like to hear them in front of a
> proper court.[172]

On that occasion, you were allowed home. You told your son
Christoph and your son-in-law, a pastor called Georg Binder,
what had happened, and they responded with an accusation of
defamation against Ursula Reinbold. This was the beginning of
several years of ugly wrangling, in which the two families, the
Keplers and the Reinbolds, would each seek to protect the reputation of one of their female members by blackening the reputation
of a woman from the other family. For a woman's character to be
up for public discussion was already shameful enough in itself.

The scope for public discussion of a woman's character has
broadened since your time, and in ways that even your far-
thinking son would have strained to imagine. These days
anyone with access to the right devices can disseminate their
opinion of anyone else across the world in a fraction of a second.
Inevitably, most of these utterances get drowned out by the
general noise – just as they would if everyone in Leonberg gathered in the town square and all started talking loudly at once

– but if words are sharp enough, they can still slice their way through the clamour.

Some years ago, for a brief time, I had my own voice amplified through monthly bulletins – blog posts – pasted up in one of these collectively imagined town squares, the *Psychology Today* website, where I shared thoughts about my experience of obsessive compulsive disorder. I didn't enjoy this work very much, it didn't pay, and I gave up for good after a few months, when I posted what I meant to be a tongue-in-cheek Christmas piece on the 'advantages' of obsessiveness and got pulled to bits in the public comments by someone who said that my post disgusted them. I understood from this that I was not allowed to choose the tone in which I could approach my own condition; I accepted the correction. It also provided me with the perfect excuse to give up on a commission I'd found burdensome from the start.

That wasn't the end of it, though – you can't suppress internet (global imaginary-yet-somehow-also-real town square) content once it's out there, especially if it's on a site over which you have no editorial control. For some time after I gave up posting, I continued to get notifications in my electronic inbox telling me that someone had made a comment on one or other of my posts. The vast majority of these related to my most viewed post, a piece about compulsive skin-picking which had received thousands of hits, and so many comments that some contributors had begun to refer to its page as a 'forum'. I was proud of that: proud of the fact that so many people had felt seen by my post, and that they were able to use the comment space as a place to help each other. I was able to use one or two of the suggestions myself and was grateful for them. I only wished that I could help the people who posted when they were at the end of their tethers, desperate for support, seeking suggestions for therapies, practitioners, medication – *anything*.

Over the months, the comments slowed; after a few years, they stopped altogether. Then, a few months ago, some eight years after I'd written my last post, I got a notification. It reported that a comment had appeared, not on the compulsive-picking post this time, but on another, a piece I would still redirect people to occasionally, about my difficulty earning a living and how that affected my sense of myself in a society which equates adulthood with financial independence, worth with productivity, and success with the accumulation of money. It was the first and only comment that article had ever received. I clicked through. It read, simply:

STFU

I knew what it stood for: Shut the Fuck Up.

I couldn't tell you who wrote it – the username was intentionally uninformative – and I couldn't tell you why, but I can tell you what I immediately assumed:

a) that it was written by a man
b) that it was an instruction to me as a woman.

It isn't that women are never unkind to other women – Ursula Reinbold wasn't exactly kind to you – but I had good reason for my assumptions. It conformed to a pattern of behaviour which certain men exhibit towards women who put words, or images, or anything at all up on the internet. Presumably some of these are the same men who think that when women appear outside the home, it must be for the sole purpose of providing them with objects for comment and conversation: 'Cheer up, love', 'Oi, dog!', 'Did you see the tits on her?' etc., etc. Online, these dashing blades are joined by men who don't have the confidence for street-harassment, but feel emboldened to throw out a passing 'STFU' or 'Ugly bitch' or 'You should be raped' when they can hide at home, behind an anonymous username and a cartoon avatar. Feminist writer Mona Eltahawy has identified the Trifecta of Misogyny: Street, State, Home.[173] The internet brings the misogyny of the street into the home. The fact that women in my part of the world, and in yours, are no longer subject to the official, state-sanctioned, religiously coded policing of behaviour and demeanour which restricted your life and shaped your fate, doesn't mean that we're not still policed, and quite harshly – it's just that the work's been taken over by enthusiastic amateurs.

It was unnecessary, actually, for the internet to have sent me that explicit instruction: STFU. By the time the message came through, I had been obeying it, more often than not, for years. I was not born obedient: like that of most autistics, my own uncorrected speech strikes most people as disconcertingly blunt, as I imagine yours must have done. But since my birth, I have been subject to fifty years of correction. Sometimes the correction was explicit, such as the time when I was twelve and allowed to join the grown-ups' dinner party. I thought I was on good form – I got lots of laughs – but after the last guest had gone, my mother tore strips off me for taking up so much attention; she had not been able to have the conversation she had meant to have with someone she hadn't spoken to for a very long time, and this was my fault. I remember that evening very well, because it was the beginning of a lifelong habit of what psychologists call 'social scanning' – retrospective rumination on a social encounter, feeling out the remembered texture of the encounter for knots and bumps and fraying tissue. For decades after that dinner party, whenever I met someone for the first time, I would reassure myself afterwards by remembering three things I knew about them – this meant I couldn't have been talking all the time, and definitely not about me.

As I got older, I learned that it wasn't just too great a quantity of speech that was prohibited – there was also a range of other possible speech misdemeanours: wrong subject, wrong tone (like my 'disgusting' blog post), wrong timing. At my girls' school, I got explicit guidance, kindly meant but usually unsolicited, from other girls, and learned, among other things, that: I shouldn't repeatedly tell someone I admired them – it sounded creepy; I didn't talk about the little things most people liked to talk about, which made it difficult for them to get on with me; I shouldn't try too hard to please people. I learned, implicitly, that you don't make friends by always having your hand and having the right answers (not that that stopped me most of the time – I do love having a right answer) or by taking up time in A-Level English having discussions with the teacher about points irrelevant to the syllabus. I should say that I was and am grateful for the advice, even when it was painful to hear. One reason that autism in girls often presents more subtly than it does in autistic boys comes from the fact that girls will take it upon themselves to set other girls straight.

I say 'girls', though women never really grow out of correcting each other. Mothers correct their daughters, as my mother corrected me after the dinner party. Rublack mentions that one of your tasks as a mother was to ensure that your daughter Margaretha behaved herself and kept her reputation spotless until she was married, after which her reputation was presumably her husband's business. Many years later and some miles away, my mother saw it as part of her task to tell me to stand up straight (otherwise I might 'droop early'), sit with my legs together, cover my mouth when I laughed and never laugh at blue jokes in front of men. She told me not to undress with the light on because if I did I could 'get into trouble'. She wanted me to wear a slip under my thin summer school dress, which I refused to do, because the new regime of bras and sanitary towels was discomfort and misery enough – the sanitary towels, by the way, had to be kept out of the bathroom because it would be upsetting to my father to see them.

I don't want to paint my mother as some kind of villain here. She was only doing what she believed she needed to do to protect me: a watered-down, updated version of what her mother, her aunts and her grandmother had done to keep her safe and out of trouble. My uncle had had to persuade them to allow my mother to leave the house and go to university, and even then, her Auntie Yetta would take it upon herself to scrutinize her niece's letters for signs of reputation-damaging behaviour. Yetta, the youngest of my grandmother's siblings and the only one born in the UK, would sometimes tell me stories of how cruelly strict her older sisters had been towards her, how Sylvia caught her and a friend eating chips in the street one day, and what hell there had been to pay for that. Yetta would then tell me to stand up straight, get my teeth sorted out and swap my Doc Martens for more feminine shoes.

Yetta died in 1990, but I've been writing about her ever since; she haunts me. She embodies the contradiction running through all those generations of women in my mother's East-End-made-good Jewish family: the way in which they sought to enforce ladylike behaviour, while being at the same time quite subversively unladylike themselves, a tendency encapsulated beautifully by something I heard Yetta bark one wet afternoon when my mother opened the door to her: 'It's PISSING DOWN out there – [sees me, doesn't even bother to draw a breath] you didn't hear that, young lady!'

But I did hear it; I heard both parts of the utterance, equally loudly, and I'm still listening intently to their echo. Thinking back once more to that evening when Mum told me, in so many less rude words, to STFU, I'm wondering if part of her anger came from seeing a tendency in me that reminded her of something she had been taught to dislike in herself – or, at least, to feel extremely ambivalent about. For my mother was most definitely not one to STFU. I grew up listening to my mother talk – not just talk, but argue, assert, pronounce, denounce, advocate for, criticize and question – and I also grew up watching the ways other people reacted when she did. I saw people roll their eyes or exchange glances; I saw their smiles freeze; I knew that some of her in-laws saw her as 'strident', the pushy woman who wore the trousers and bossed my poor father around. My paternal grandmother didn't understand why my mother 'worked' if she didn't 'need to'; it had to be that my father couldn't provide.

Through her example, my mother taught me to speak up. Observing people's reactions to her speech taught me that speaking up came with a price. When I read the work of feminist theorist Sara Ahmed, and came across her equation

Rolling eyes = feminist pedagogy[174]

I knew at once what she meant. I remembered the rolling eyes when, for example, my mother complained that in our supposedly egalitarian Reform synagogue, women were rarely called up to read. I remembered the rolling eyes when she held forth about inequalities in the workplace. I remembered how my brother would roll his eyes when my mother and I screamed 'Sexist! That's utterly gratuitous! Did you *see* that?' at a particular British Rail advert every time it came on, until one day he snapped: 'Yes, I *know* already – do you *have* to say so every time?' We stopped saying it.

My brother was a cis-het white male, it's true, but he was also a vulnerable individual, and the youngest, quietest person in that room. Many years later, he would stop talking to my mother, and then to me, and then take his own life. In the dreadful years after his death, as I ruminated endlessly over why he might have done it and who might have been to blame, I came to see my mother's and my joint sofa campaign against that advert – such a trivial thing in itself – as emblematic of the kind of behaviour that poked at my brother's vulnerability. But as I'm writing this, I realize how absurd it's been to yoke together these two issues – my mother's and my feminism and my brother's horrible death. Perhaps the answer to his question was: 'Yes, we do have to say so every time, because every time we see another woman's body objectified, it is by implication an attack on our personhood, and when we are attacked in this way, we have every right to re-assert that personhood by refusing that objectification.'

Now that I've written that down, I wonder how I could have done that to myself all these years – nearly twelve now, since my brother died. Why was it so easy, why did it feel so natural, to blame myself and my mother for edging my brother out of existence simply by being what Ahmed calls 'pushy feminists… those feminists who refuse to let it go'?[175] I'm thinking now of your life, too, of the fact that when you were under suspicion of witchcraft, members of your own family – particularly your youngest son Christoph – speculated that it was your behaviour that had driven your husband repeatedly from your home, and led to his early death.

When Ursula Reinbold made her accusation, you most certainly didn't let it go. Nor were you content to stay back and allow your menfolk to speak for you. You tried to act for yourself, and when you did, you made mistakes. Your first was to offer Einhorn, the governor, a gift of a silver cup. There was nothing unusual in the act itself: it was common for townspeople to give their governors gifts of significant value, in the hope that this would be remembered when a judgement had to be made which concerned them. Perhaps if you had given Einhorn the gift before you were accused, it might have helped, but you presented it to him after that first meeting at his house, after he had already chosen to ignore the regulations and summoned you to face your accusers. He had already made it clear which side he was on, and your cup could only be interpreted as a bribe, in effect an acknowledgement of guilt. That you arrived at your appointment with the cup hidden under your gown, rather than presenting it straight away, only served to reinforce the impression of guilt and cunning.[176] The silver cup represented a grave error of judgement that would haunt you and your family throughout the trials that followed.

It was just one of many instances in which you had failed to read another person, and this failure had laid your own behaviour open to a damaging misreading. Like my mother, sometimes, and like me, sometimes, you seem to have had a tendency to persevere in social encounters, to persist in a course of action even after it was already beginning to cause discomfort. You insisted that the schoolteacher take a cup of wine after he had made it clear that he was on his way to church and your invitation was not welcome or convenient. You persisted in demanding milk from your neighbour even after she had told you repeatedly that she had none to spare, and had suggested a reasonable alternative course of action for you. One of the three judges who presided over your final interrogation in Leonberg agreed with a witness that what made people so suspicious was your habit of 'endlessly running about and into people's houses': even in such a close-knit community, there was still such a thing as personal space, and you appeared to be insufficiently aware of this.[177] It was mistakes like these, small in themselves but far too numerous, which helped to build up the reservoir of bad feeling that your prosecutors were able to draw on when they came to build their case.

In order to build *his* case for the defence, Johannes had to take your behavioural quirks, and their effect on others, into account. He needed to explain clearly that what might appear to be signs of unwomanly coldness displayed by a malevolent witch were actually nothing of the kind. He had to explain exactly why and how you were misunderstood. When I read your story in Rublack's book, certain recurring themes jumped out at me. In all kinds of subtle and less subtle ways, your performance of womanhood was wanting.

One of these was your inability or refusal to cry, even when threatened with torture. Ursula Reinbold's tears and vocal distress over the years which followed her first accusation consistently lent weight to her credibility as a witness and a woman wronged by witchcraft. (In a patriarchal society, the conspicuous shedding of tears can be a female power move, which more privileged women – white, middle-class, heterosexual, conventionally attractive, and so on – use to gain advantage over their less privileged, less protected counterparts.[178]) In contrast, your apparent lack of affect undermined your credibility as an innocent woman wronged by malicious accusations. Another one of the three Leonberg judges remarked that, although you seemed shocked by the charges, you had not 'shed a single tear'. As Rublack explains, this meant that you were judged to be 'uncanny in a culture whose theologians increasingly demanded that hearts needed to be moved... [and] proclaimed that natural disasters were controlled by an angry God who wanted his children to cry for mercy.'[179] For women, tears were also seen as a sign of tender, motherly love – the kind that Heinrich had accused you of lacking. This is Rublack's description of you at the Leonberg hearing:

> Katharina did not want to comply with men's idea of when and how she should express emotion. Although she was addressed by the judge as 'Cathy' (*Cätherlin*), and the judge finally spoke to her in more familiar terms, saying 'if you have a pious drop of blood in yourself, then let your eyes flow', Katharina replied: 'I have cried so much, that now I cannot cry any more'. Next, she promised to shout for revenge at the Day of Judgement. She felt angry, not sad. She would not break down. Refusing to cry, in all likelihood, was her way of retaining dignity and strength to live through the rest of the trial.[180]

When Kepler put forward his defence, he offered a medical explanation for your lack of tears, claiming that tears could sometimes naturally dry up, especially in a person as old his mother. Other sources of suspicion, which required explanation, were your lack of eye contact and a lack of facial expressiveness. It was noted that you did not meet any of the witnesses' eyes as they

testified, a failure which was seen as indicative of a lack of compassion as well as guilt. The judge who remarked on your lack of
tears also recorded that, when faced by witnesses, you had kept
'looking down or to the side... [your] eyes moving unsteadily'.[181]
Johannes, who knew you so well and spoke at length to you
during your period of imprisonment to draw out your version
of events, was able to make his own 'evaluation of [your] way of
showing or concealing emotions'.

> It was her nature, he argued, not to show many facial
> expressions, no matter whether she was happy or serious,
> but especially when she argued. She never looked into
> anyone's eyes when quarrelling, but faced them from the
> side, as she tried to focus her thoughts. Kepler emphasised
> that his mother was bold and fearless in her readiness to
> stand up to anyone challenging her. She typically dealt
> with unfair comments by warding them off with gestures
> and words. No one, he summed up, would ever have seen
> his mother cry.[182]

I really felt for you when I read this. I also find it hard to maintain eye contact and focus my thoughts at the same time. And
like you, my feelings often fail to show in my face in a way that
most people can recognize, or at least, they fail to show quickly
enough. One of the many things I've learned in my long, not
entirely successful career as a student of performative womanhood is that there is no such thing as an acceptable resting face
when that face is on a woman. Even when we're walking down
the street by ourselves, minding our own business, we're supposed to project a kind of positive social receptivity on standby.
If you fail to signal that you are ready at any moment to employ

your facial muscles to help create a pleasing and reassuring social environment for everyone in the vicinity, then you have to be a miserable bitch.

My current autism reading is a book by Gordon Gates, a Canadian counsellor who is himself autistic. It's called *Trauma, Stigma, and Autism: Developing Resilience and Loosening the Grip of Shame*.[183] The trauma he discusses is not 'shock trauma' of the kind you must have experienced when you were seized and taken to prison, or that I experienced when I miscarried in a rush of blood and it felt as if the bleeding might never stop. It's trauma of the subtler kind, experienced as a result of a less tangible kind of peril. When the concept of a traumatic experience was first formulated, a trauma response was understood to arise only in the wake of direct threats to one's physical being, to the integrity and survival of the physical body, but over the years its scope has widened to acknowledge threats to the integrity and survival of the self. There are countless definitions of trauma to choose from, but my favourite is this one from Juliet Mitchell, because she succeeds so well in conveying that truth that, whether physical or psychical, a trauma is always experienced as something which ruptures the self, and overwhelms its usual capacities for self-defence:

A trauma, whether physical or psychical, must create a breach in a protective covering of such severity that it cannot be coped with by the usual mechanisms by which we deal with pain or loss.[184]

Judith Lewis Herman, whose book *Trauma and Recovery* did so much to open up the concept of trauma and widen it beyond its traditional association with shell shock, explains the 'usual mechanisms' by which a human being deals with danger as a 'complex, integrated system of reactions, encompassing both body and mind'.[185] The sympathetic nervous system is aroused, causing a rush of adrenalin. These physiological processes put the individual in an alert state, in which they concentrate on the perceived threat, sometimes to an extent that allows them to ignore the body's signals of 'hunger, fatigue or pain'. The physical effects are accompanied by feelings of fear and anger. As Herman explains, these 'changes in arousal, attention, perception, and emotion are normal adaptive reactions. They mobilize the threatened person for strenuous action, either in battle or in flight.'[186] Under the right conditions, this is a state designed to produce the right behaviour, actions designed to promote survival. However, when 'action is of no avail' and 'neither resistance nor escape is possible',[187] traumatic reactions occur. In a traumatized individual, the responses of body and mind which work so well together when a dangerous situation can be resolved, persist in their unresolved state after the initial situation is over, and persist in a fragmented, disorganized fashion: trauma survivors can be haunted by splinters of memory devoid of feeling or context, bursts of overwhelming negative feeling with no obvious cause, compulsions to flee or fight or freeze which they cannot control and struggle to explain. Trauma breaks apart the unities of time and place which we rely on for a usual narrative sense of self. A traumatic story is a story that resists being told, to oneself or to others.

All traumatic experience confounds communication; Gates focuses on a sub-type of psychical trauma which can be especially slippery to identify and to describe. Sometimes referred to as 'complex' or 'developmental' trauma, it builds up slowly, over years, the result of attrition from repeated insults to a person's sense of self, security and integrity. The individual insults may be small, almost imperceptibly small, but if they take place frequently enough, and over a sufficiently long time, their cumulative effect can be severe.

As the word 'developmental' implies, this is a kind of trauma which is often experienced in the earliest years of life. Gates alludes to the psychologist John Bowlby's attachment theory, in which he set out the idea that inconsistency or too much distance or various other kinds of 'disturbances of emotional attachment'[188] between an infant and their primary caregiver (for which, of course, read 'mother') could result in lifelong difficulties involving unstable emotional states, compulsive patterns of behaviour and problems in relating to others. As Gates explains, 'Such threats to the safety and security of growing children due to a lack of consistently supportive caregiver attention have been shown to better predict extreme symptoms of emotional dysregulation and mental health distress in adults than the severity of various other forms of abuse'.[189] Just to be clear: even if a child is physically safe – fed, cleaned, sheltered, competently handled, not deliberately harmed – certain kinds of disturbance in their relationship with their caregivers can result in a failure to experience their environment as safe. Attachment theory can too easily segue into mother-blaming, so I want you to understand that this lack of a sense of safety doesn't have to be the caregiver's (read 'mother's') fault; a parent and a baby are two different people, and sometimes, with the best will in the world, two people can be a bad fit for each other. Misrecognition is very often mutual.

Gates talks about the 'ethics of encounter' that come into play in any interpersonal relationship, about the responsibility to recognize the other person's subjectivity and personhood, even if their way of expressing it is very different from your own. There is a difference between simply attending to a person's physical needs and caring for that person, with all that the word implies, and when you're on the receiving end, you can feel that difference. It's something to do with the presence or absence of emotional reciprocity and receptiveness. I can recall times in my own life when I've been competently but briskly handled, by a parent or a healthcare worker or a teacher – we've all experienced these moments and we've all probably inflicted them too – and I've definitely felt that difference. It's the difference between being met as a person and being dealt with like a thing. Gates's term for the effect of cumulative 'attacks on [one's] personhood' is 'invalidation trauma'.[190]

This need to be met, to be respected and nurtured as a fellow human being, does not cease to be important after we've emerged from infancy, and if it is not met, we can never feel quite safe. Even if we were loved as infants, and feel that we were loved, we continue to need the human world to meet us as people, and when it does not, when instead it deals with us as if we were things, it hurts. Any autistic person will be miserably familiar with this experience of failing to be met, of being distanced and dealt with. All too often, when non-autistic people encounter us, and register all the subtle and less subtle differences in our self-presentation, our speech, our demeanour, our facial expressions, our body language, our social behaviour, these seem somehow to add up to the impression of a being other than human, with whom there can be no consistent emotional reciprocity, no mutual receptiveness, no shared first person plural.

This judgement as often as not happens unconsciously, and in the blink of an eye, but once it's been made, its object is placed firmly in the third person, and more often than not she stays there. It's a moment of social misrecognition followed swiftly by one of social negation, and you know when it's happened: you can feel the person flinch from you, even if they don't appear to move a millimetre. That person does not feel comfortable with you, and you cannot feel sure of being safe with them. And that's just from a microflinch. There are worse experiences, common to most autistic people and some most familiar to autistic women, and often involving more than one person: bullying, the overt or covert ostracism and rejection, the open mockery, the angry or righteous corrections that sometimes seem to come out of nowhere, the predatory behaviour of men who can sense naivety and vulnerability and seek to take advantage. Once you have been pushed outside the first person plural, anything might be done to you, anything might happen. You had an entire town gang up on you.

As these adverse experiences, big and small, build up during our childhoods and then continue to build up over our lifetimes, we accumulate these traumas, these countless breaches in our protective covering, and this has a further deforming effect on the way we see ourselves and the way we relate to others. Sometimes it's not that easy to distinguish autism and post-traumatic stress; often, they are closely intertwined.

It is a rare autistic individual whose personality has not in some way been shaped through their response to trauma. A person who is constantly anticipating danger – who is in a resting state of 'hyperarousal' – will be someone who is always ready to flee, fight or freeze. Or they might incline towards another form of trauma response, the 'Fourth F' known as 'fawning'. This last F is a relatively new concept, and it's not easy to find a reliable-sounding definition, but I came across a simple and clear explanation of all Four Fs in a book by Pete Walker, called *Complex PTSD: From Thriving to Surviving: A Guide and Map for Recovering from Childhood Trauma*:

> A fight response is triggered when a person suddenly responds aggressively to something threatening. A flight response is triggered when a person responds to a perceived threat by fleeing, or symbolically, by launching into hyperactivity. A freeze response is triggered when a person, realizing resistance is futile, gives up, numbs out into dissociation and/or collapses as if accepting the inevitability of being hurt. A fawn response is triggered when a person responds to threat by trying to be pleasing and helpful in order to forestall an attacker.[191]

I wondered if Walker had anything to say about how differences in socialization between men and women might affect how they responded to adverse experiences, and I was glad to see that he does. In his chapter on grieving, he notes that 'Many of us suffer from a socialization process that relegates angering [*sic*] to men and crying to women. From an early age boys are shamed for crying while girls are treated similarly for angering.'[192] This seems a sufficient explanation for why there are so many men who react to sadness with anger and violence, and so many women who express anger through tears and complaint. The way you were vilified for standing your ground and arguing and refusing to cry suggests that, in this respect at least, little has changed between your time and mine.

I can remember being shamed for being angry, for actively refusing to do things or for expressing my frustration or discomfort in ways that were seen as inappropriate. There was the day when I was four years old and I refused to put on any of the fussy, uncomfortable dresses my mother wanted me to wear to go to some family do or other. I don't remember how I shouted 'No!' again and again; what I do remember is a floor covered in dresses, my mother in tears, and my father saying, 'Look, now you've made Mummy cry...' Apparently I was so shocked by the scene that I stopped resisting and stood, quietly and passively, while my mother manoeuvred me into the first fussy dress I'd refused. I submitted, on that occasion, to the doll life, to quiet and prettiness.

I remember another moment, this time in the second year of junior school. It wasn't the worst moment in that year by any means (that was the year in which all the other girls in the class ganged up on me and went to the supply teacher with false accusations about my lunch-eating habits – you'll understand what that felt like), but was another moment when I was shamed. I was making some art project. It involved stapling shapes together to make a dome. I'm very cack-handed, but I hadn't yet learned to accept that I was or to be patient with myself about it. I believed that I had to do well at everything and I had to do well at speed; I thought that was what being me meant. So I didn't slow down. I didn't put my hand up to ask for help. Instead I pushed on, making a mess of it, wrestling with the cardboard and the stapler until, at the peak of my frustration, I erupted with a roar and pushed the whole lot – cardboard, stapler – off my desk and onto the floor.

Jo-ANNE! Don't be like that! You mustn't lose your temper!

Some of the good girls around me echoed this, as good girls know to do. Some of the boys around me sniggered.

In that moment of humiliation, I was angry with the teacher and angry with the class. But as time went on, and I grew older, and I got corrected, and I watched my mother, and I learned, I came to see the incident as one of those in which other people's adverse reactions were entirely my own fault, for not making the effort to soften myself. When I stand back and look at it all together – Ahmed and Eltahawy on feminism and misogyny, Gates and Walker on trauma, the way in which autistic girls slip quietly under the radar, your story, the story of the women in my family, my own story – I can see all the ways in which autism, gender and invalidation trauma twine around each other.

The code of behaviour our society sets out for girls and women is so much more detailed and complex than the code handed out to men. Girls get corrected more often, and for smaller and subtler infractions, and it doesn't stop when they become women. It is assumed that, as females, we are naturally better at picking up on social conventions, naturally better at anticipating needs, and naturally better at meeting them without letting on that we are engaged in this labour. We are supposed to know how people are without asking them and then engineer the shared social space accordingly. There's a deceptively simple term for all this subtle, complex work in the white middle-class milieu I was socialized in – we call it 'niceness'.

When it comes to niceness and the expectation of social and emotional effort that the word represents for me, it seems obvious that men are simply not held to the same standards. We all know abrupt men, argumentative men, awkward men, men who dominate the room without thinking, men who habitually centre any conversation around their own interests and talk about them at length, anti-social men who always leave the room – we accept them and, if they are sufficiently successful, or clever or talented or powerful, we may even respect their lack of niceness as part of the mystique of the successful, clever, talented, powerful man. We appreciate it if a man is nice, but it's not an essential criterion in the person spec for being a man. In the person spec for being a woman, it always seemed to me to be one of the most essential: if you fail to meet it, you experience all those traumas, mostly little but sometimes not so little, that come from failing to conform to social expectations, from all the hostility, the correction and rejection, the various humiliations, which follow that failure; you bank up fear, you bank up anger, you bank up shame, you bank up all manner of physiological, psychological and interpersonal trouble. And it's worse when you can't find the words for why…

… then when you do finally find the words, and with them a way to tell that previously untellable trauma story, it's like being given the keys to a prison you'd never even realized you were living in.

I should probably STFU about prison, though. I don't have any lived experience. Where prison's concerned, the epistemic privilege – the most unenviable epistemic privilege – is all yours.

There were six years between Ursula Reinbold's initial denunciation and your final hearing. I find all the twists and turns of the case difficult enough to follow as a reader, so I can barely imagine how bewildering and stressful it must have been to live through them. There seem to have been numerous hearings, arguments, petitions and counter-petitions, decisions by ducal governors and ducal courts, periods when you were under arrest followed by periods when you were not, trips to shelter with your daughter Margaretha in Heumaden near Leonberg and your son Johannes in Linz, much further away.

So the case dragged on and on, the arguments went back and forth, until finally, in the summer of 1620, five years since Ursula Reinbold's original outburst, you were arrested and taken to prison to await trial. The circumstances were particularly humiliating. You were staying with your daughter. The guards from Stuttgart arrived, abruptly and unexpectedly, in the early hours of the morning. When the servants woke the family to tell them, Margaretha was dressed only in a smock, and you had nothing on at all. Margaretha, in her panic, told you to hide in a trunk and that's where they found you, in your nakedness, hunched up and shivering with fear.

You were allowed to dress, before you were held briefly in Stuttgart and then taken to Leonberg, where you were interrogated by Einhorn, the local pastor, and several judges – this was the point at which you were tested on your knowledge of religion, and acquitted yourself well. Ever honest to a fault, you admitted that you had once 'received the host in a Catholic mass',[193] but although you had dealt with Catholics, you refuted any suggestion that you had also had dealings with the devil. Alone, with no legal guardian to speak for you, you then had to face a large group of local witnesses – seventeen in all – and respond to their accusations. At one point you acknowledged that you had recommended a blessing to the local butcher, and were able to recite it, to show that it was indeed a blessing, and not a spell:

God be welcome to me
On Sun- and sunny days.
You come riding towards us,
There stands a human, let yourself be asked,
God, Father, Son and Holy Ghost,
And the Holy Trinity,
Give this person blood and flesh
As well as good health.[194]

You explained that you saw this as a prayer and had used it when your own children were ill. Mention of your children reminded the hostile witnesses of Heinrich's accusations against you, and you explained how much trouble he had caused you: how you had taken care of one of his abandoned daughters, how roughly he had spoken to you, how you had rebuked him when he converted to Catholicism. You admitted that you had at times spoken very sharply yourself, responding with 'angry sarcasm' towards attacks on your reputation. For example, there was the time when you had 'told a man who called [you] a witch that [you] would "show him" and make bad weather. But these had just been words.'[195] It was during this process, as you concentrated intently and had to marshal rational arguments to meet your accusations, that the jury noted your lack of tears, and of eye contact.

After the hearing was over, a report was sent to the ducal chancellors in Stuttgart. It concluded with an allegation that you knew a woman from Eltingen who had been accused of witchcraft in 1616. That was a downright lie, but it must have helped to convince the chancellors, because they told Governor Einhorn to give you a verbal warning that you were under threat of torture, and to use the threat to try and get you to confess. This you refused to do, so you were formally charged – something which Einhorn had failed to do for some five years – and imprisoned, on the understanding that you were to face torture for real. You were first imprisoned in Leonberg, but following a complaint from your son Christoph, who was concerned about the effect on his own reputation and hard-won civic dignity, you were transferred to Güglingen.

Margaretha sent word to Johannes in Linz. After writing a furious letter to the Duke, he packed up his household and came to Württemberg. By the time he reached you, you had already spent three weeks behind bars. He found you cold and miserable in the prison tower, not only physically uncomfortable but also very lonely, as Margaretha, your main source of comfort, had just moved away with her husband to a new parish some 18 miles from Stuttgart. Johannes was shocked to see your living conditions. He requested that you be moved from the tower to the quarters of the civic guard, where you could be kept more comfortably, explaining that you would be able to pay. As all your assets had been seized, he also insisted that Einhorn release an amount of money sufficient for your immediate needs.

Rather than agree to these reasonable measures to make a frail old woman more comfortable, the chancellery and the civic guard held a full discussion. The civic guard said that his property was too small to accommodate a prisoner and, besides, he had young children – he was not prepared to live under the same roof as you. There was further disagreement among the chancellors, not only about where you should be held but how: how many guards should watch you? Should you be chained? After some lengthy wrangling, which threatened to continue into the darker, colder winter months, it was agreed that you should be 'moved to a room on the upper floor of one of Güglingen's town gates, fastened by an iron chain, and watched by one guard'.[196]

The presence of a guard was no mere formality; nor was he there only to prevent you from walking out. The local governor, Aulber, no more your friend than Einhorn, saw to it that even in prison every detail of your speech and conduct could be scrutinized for further signs of guilt which might be passed to the prosecution. When you teased a guard for not leaving the door open while he fetched water for you, joking that 'you are such a bad man, that you do not at all trust me', Aulber interpreted it as an attempt to soften the guard up in preparation for a break-out.[197] There were some occasions when the guards themselves were suspicious, such as the time when one came in with food and asked what you were doing, and you apparently answered: 'But what am I to do: I am lying here. Dear man, dear man, let me out, I will give you 100 florins in money, and if I don't give you the money I shall give you a letter (of exchange) for 100 florins.'[198] If this was meant to be a joke, it misfired terribly: the guards, far from amused, began to question you about where this money would come from. First, you denied having said anything; then you confessed that a fellow prisoner in Leonberg had given you the money before her execution. What your son described as your 'clumsy manner' with people continued to tell against you.

As I write this letter, I'm living under conditions which seem strange to me and my contemporaries, but would probably be more recognizable to you and yours. We are living through a time of sickness, the like of which we have not seen for at least a century; modern medicine, which has spared us so much during that century, has not yet developed the means to stop this new sickness spreading, or killing a significant proportion of the people who contract it. Our government has responded by limiting everyone's movements, our contacts with each other. We are not to travel. We are only to leave our homes for specific reasons, and we can be reprimanded, or questioned, or reported, or even fined, if we are found to be breaking these rules. People have seen their livelihoods shrink or disappear. People in poor health are housebound, and sometimes dependent on the good will of their neighbours to stay alive. That sense of the uncertainty and precariousness of life, which a few weeks ago was confined to the poor and the chronically ill, and which most people were only too happy to ignore, has emerged from its ghetto and become general.

There is a test for this sickness, but only a few people have taken it. As for the rest of us, we don't know who might infect us and we don't know who we might infect. (I think I may have had a mild case myself a few weeks ago, but I have no way of being sure.) Some people wear masks, though these are not yet mandatory. When we leave the house, we are supposed to keep at least two metres between ourselves and anyone who doesn't live with us. This is easier in some places than others. In a park, it's easy. In a small local supermarket, such as the one I visit every two or three days, it isn't. The aisles are not much more than two metres long, and quite a lot less than two metres wide, so if you want to enter one, and someone else is already there, you have to hover at the end of the aisle until they've moved on.

I went to the shop this morning. I needed something from the cat food, cleaning and toiletries aisle, and there was a man hovering in front of the pet food. He started to move away. I started to move forwards. Then he stopped. I stopped. Then he moved again. I started to move. Then he stopped. I stopped. He looked over his shoulder at me; there was a tiny sense of discomfort, and I felt compelled to dissipate it. I smiled my Nice Lady Smile and, in my Nice Lady Voice With a Smile In It, I said, 'It's hard to know what to do, isn't it?' He smiled back and agreed with me. I'd succeeded in popping a minuscule bubble of social tension and it was almost physically gratifying, like popping a pimple.

Skin imperfections, imperfections of the social encounter. I've told you how I'll scan an encounter for social blunders, feeling out 'the remembered texture of the encounter for knots and bumps and fraying tissue'. I could just as easily have been talking about the way I run my hand over my skin before I start picking it, a miserable habit which has resulted in far more damage and blemishes than I ever would have had if I'd often left my skin alone. As for the social scanning, what I've realized from my aisle story is that I've now learned to do it not only in retrospect, but also in real time. Scanning and trouble-shooting in real time – sometimes scanning and trouble-shooting pre-emptively – I'm able to do a passable impression of the 'nice', i.e. socially gracious, sort of woman it feels safest for me to be.

Sometimes, the creation of that socially gracious persona has felt like the greatest and most worthwhile creative achievement of my life, but now I wonder if, like my skin-picking, like all the obsessive compulsive ruminations and avoidances which promised to keep me safe, her creation and maintenance hasn't, in the end, harmed at least as much as it's helped. It isn't just the traumatic experience itself that causes the damage – it's also the Four Fs, the armour we adopt to stop it from happening again, the armour that pinches and weighs us down, that cramps our movements, that forms an inflexible barrier between ourselves and others, the protective visor that eats into the face.

This image of a suit of armour puts me in mind of other rigid garments, the ones associated with femininity rather than masculinity: the boned corsets, the shapewear, the bras that take unruly parts of one's person and then move and restrain them so as to make sure that they do not deviate in their position, their shape or their movement; garments that control; garments that correct. Socially Gracious Joanne (SGJ) is a rigid container for an unruly social self. Her underpinnings are made out of explicit corrections – Don't-Sit-Like-That; Don't-Look-Like-That; Don't-Talk-Like-That; Don't-Move-Like-That. They are made from what I have learned by pre- and proscription. Her made-to-please covering consists of fragments of other women's dress sense, tone of voice, demeanour, facial expressions, gestures and turns of phrase. It is made from what I've learned by example.

The decision to make SGJ was never entirely conscious – that's not how trauma defences come about – and neither was her ongoing construction and maintenance. That said, I do remember a point where I consciously decided to change. It was after three years of hanging on miserably at university – if I had valued myself and my well-being more than I valued keeping my status and saving my face, I would have left after the first term. In the first year, I had fucked up royally, socially as well as academically: I got rejected, a lot, and, to a lesser extent, bullied. I felt lost and terrified all the time, but apparently I was intimidating. I did not know how to look after myself, or manage my time, and found the shared accommodation unbearably noisy. I missed tutorials; I failed to hand in essays. I overslept and almost missed one of my exams. In the second and third years I had shut everything down and shrunk inside myself, hoping that at least I could come out with a degree. I worked just enough and complained too much, exhausting a lot of people's patience. I got a degree, but I didn't know what to do with it, or myself. I came to the conclusion there was no doing anything with myself as I was. I was repulsive to myself and fairly sure that I was repulsive to other people too, particularly male people (a serious problem for a straight girl). For my sake and everybody else's, I would have to change. I wrote a diary, itemizing my faults, where I denounced myself as a 'failed girl', and told myself to start again.

I started doing sit-ups and flattened my stomach. I could not afford to leave my parental home, but I found the first of many short-lived jobs, commuted and received a tiny pay packet every month, which felt like a small step towards real personhood. I started a distance learning course in Creative Writing so that I could learn that properly, from the beginning. On Mondays after work, I went to a poetry workshop at City University; on Wednesdays after work I went to a centre in Queen's Park which offered therapy to young people, at rates which young people with tiny pay packets could afford.

As I said, I couldn't say for sure what SGJ's origin story might be, but that post-university year provides as good a starting point as any. There's a neat twenty-year gap between that decision to change and the autism diagnosis I received at forty-two, which gave me a number of new ways to understand SGJ, and prompted me to rethink my relationship with her.

From one perspective, you could see her as entirely positive, useful and helpful: she protects me from adverse social experiences, and she also embodies my sincere desire that I should not make other people uncomfortable just by being myself. I care about other people's feelings – that's a good thing, isn't it? SGJ is adaptive. If she were the outcome of a formal course of Applied Behavioural Analysis (ABA; a common form of therapeutic intervention for early-diagnosed autistic people; think of 'conversion therapy', except, instead of turning gay people straight, it makes awkward people easier to be around), then that course would be counted a success.

If you were an autism researcher writing a paper exploring why the diagnosis of autistic girls typically happens so much later than it does for boys, you would talk in terms of 'masking' or 'camouflaging'. On the one hand, you would see SGJ as representing an advantage which girls have over boys, in our capacity to develop social skills, adopt working models of appropriate behaviour and fit in (good girls!). On the other hand, you would see her as representing a problem in that our development of such personas causes us to 'fly under the radar' and so lose out on appropriate support. This assumes, of course, that such support is available – it frequently isn't.

Or you might consider her as a product of trauma, as an incoherent, fragmented structure, designed to offer protection to an incoherent, fragmented, otherwise armourless self. It is true that, in part, she is made out of echoes of traumatic experience, out of hurtful acts of correction. Anna Freud wrote a celebrated paper about the way in which powerless people sometimes defend themselves internally by identifying with their aggressors, with those who wield power over them.[199] She was writing, post-war, about the experience of Jews under Nazism, but the idea holds for less extreme situations too. Think of a little girl telling off her doll. When I'm being SGJ, I'm both the little girl and the doll. In terms of the traumatic Four Fs, she is part Freeze, for her passivity; as a decoy to cover my retreat, she is part Flight; in her people-pleasing design, she is Fawn.

Then again, if you were a disability theorist or activist, you would understand the creation and maintenance of SGJ as something that allows me to 'pass' as able, or – to use a word I've come to hate – 'normal'. When I inhabit the persona of SGJ successfully, my autism, my difference or disability, becomes barely visible. This grants me the 'passing privilege' by which I can move through the world with the relative social ease of the able, privately educated, middle-class, white female Oxbridge graduate I would be if I were not autistic. And even allowing for the Jewishness which is also invisible to most people, that's a high degree of social ease. And even allowing for the fact this it is conditional upon my passing for something I am not, that's a lot of privilege.

SGJ is a complex, even paradoxical figure, at once the embodiment of both my disability and of the privileges which protect me from so many of the consequences of being disabled. On the one hand, she is exhausting to run, and drains resources from me, resources which I might otherwise use to be the best version of my autistic self rather than an inferior version of a non-autistic woman. And SGJ is in some respects a lousy piece of kit: she doesn't always work, she has limited spontaneity and almost no initiative, she can't always quite fit herself to the situations she finds herself in, and anyone who's around her for long enough will start to notice the joins and hear the creaking.

On the other hand, I have come to realize that SGJ would not be available to me at all were I not white and middle-class. Not long ago, I had a conversation with one of my autistic writer friends, Kate Fox. We had just recorded a podcast together and were discussing the contrast between our two voices: mine middle-class, North London RP, hers working-class and Northern. Kate said that sometimes she found it useful to draw on the persona of the bolshie, strong Northern woman, and talked about a time she'd successfully sent food back in a pub. I said I couldn't do that, that I couldn't cope with overt conflict, even on so tiny a scale. I said that I had learned that if I couldn't let something go, I would have to simper a bit and say things like 'Sorry, but...' or 'I hope you don't mind but...' or 'Oh, but I thought that...', resolve the situation that way, and then be effusively thankful and sorry for the trouble when that person corrected the mistake they shouldn't have made in the first place. And keep praising everything else. And leave them a huge tip. It was only as we were talking that it occurred to me that my gracious, smiling way with serving staff came out of a middle-class confidence that of course I was entitled to be served, and that all parties must naturally agree.

SGJ is middle-class, and SGJ is white. Reading work by women of colour has made this particular aspect starkly visible to me; privilege is, by definition, whatever one is able to leave unexamined and take for granted, and I have to acknowledge that, until relatively recently, I've avoided examining my whiteness. Minna Salami is a writer whose dual heritage – Finnish and Nigerian – enables her to examine norms of feminine behaviour from a variety of perspectives. In her book *Sensuous Knowledge: A Black Feminist Approach for Everyone*, she charts a long, painful and complicated battle to free herself from the restrictive behavioural norms imposed by 'the God Authority, the White Authority, then the Male Authority, later the Society Authority, then the Family Authority'.[200] Growing up in Nigeria, '[her] upbringing taught [her] that God was white and male', that white men discovered Africa, and 'that girls should be nice even when boys misbehaved because they were "being boys"'. A temporary move to Sweden with her mother taught her that 'Africans were uncivilized and primitive' and that her 'brown skin and bushy hair were considered unattractive'.[201] For non-white women, even those as privileged as Salami, inhabiting the persona of the approved, accepted Socially Gracious Woman in order to move through white-dominated space involves working harder for a less reliable result. And, as writers such as Sara Ahmed, Mona Eltahawy and Salami point out, a woman of colour is never further away from social ease and acceptance than when she is calling out racism, sexism or their blended manifestation, misogynoir. Calling out can mean lost relationships, lost friendships, lost opportunities.

However, as Salami came to realize, it is not just about calling out, and being what Ahmed calls a 'feminist killjoy':

The problem patriarchal society has with women is not when we oppose patriarchy intellectually but rather precisely when we act according to our opposition emotionally. It is much more acceptable for a woman to speak out against patriarchal norms, such as women being the ones who create space for intimacy in a relationship, than for her to actively stop taking responsibility for that work.[202]

It is not easy to actively stop taking responsibility for any of the emotional tasks we undertake; it is not easy to stop taking responsibility for other people's social comfort. Women of colour have to work harder than white women if they are to meet this unspoken responsibility, if they are to move through the world, socially and professionally, without encountering difficulties, without being treated as if they themselves *were* the difficulties (as Ahmed says, to draw attention to the problem is to be identified *as* the problem). Salami writes about how, over time, the distance between the self she presented to the world and the self she knew herself to be became unbearably painful. She writes: 'To avoid the constant battle between my truth and my socialization, I sensed myself slipping into the adult life that I'd once dreaded – a life shaped by others' expectations. I was too insecure and terrified to do anything about it.'[203] Eventually, she came to the realization that this work of fitting in was harming her, that it was not worth it, and was able to turn her energies to the work of freeing herself.

SGJ is middle-class. SGJ is white. SGJ can pass for neurotypical. The protection she affords would not be available to me if I were unable to speak, or to suppress the characteristics which mark me out as other. In a post on their blog Cussin' and Discussin', Mel Baggs explained that, in a society which judges people by their ability to conform to an emotionally muffled, verbally indirect, distinctly middle-class mode of relating, people with developmental disabilities must always be at a terrible disadvantage:

> People with developmental disabilities may find it harder to pretend we are feeling something we are not. We might find it harder to detach ourselves from what we are feeling. We might find it harder to act as if we don't notice something that is happening. We are sometimes more direct or blunt in our communication styles than usual. We might find it hard to act like someone is our social better, even if we are trying to be respectful. We might find it hard to speak indirectly or abstractly about something we are feeling *right now*. We might find it hard to speak *at all* if we are feeling strongly and may communicate through other means. We might find it hard to pretend we perceive the world differently than we do. We might find it hard to be abstract about something that's very concrete to us.[204]

This is a passage from a post entitled 'Nice Lady Therapists and their war against human emotion'. The term 'Nice Lady Therapist' was coined by another autistic blogger, Rabbi Ruti Regan, as a way of describing certain female professionals who harm the children they are supposed to be helping, who inflict 'invalidation trauma', but do so in ways so subtle, and so generally acceptable, that they may not even be aware they are doing it themselves.

The Nice Lady Therapists will tell their charges that 'whatever they do to us is by definition nice, and good for us. And that we like it, and that they love us, and that they are rescuing us, and that we are grateful.' They work in brightly coloured therapy rooms, in sessions filled with toys and praise and rewards and smiles, and yet 'every interaction with them is degrading in a way that's hard to pinpoint, and hard to recover from'. These interactions include treating a child as if they were younger than they are; forcing a child to do something frightening or painful while forbidding them to 'express pain or fear', as it hurts their feelings to see a child upset; sometimes 'it's a matter of being expected to accept intensely bad advice as though it's insight', such as being told that the way to make friends is to try harder with the kids who are rejecting and bullying them; sometimes it's even touching a child invasively and against their expressed wishes, while telling them it must be for their own good, because by definition anything the Nice Lady Therapist says or does is good and nice and nurturing.[205]

When I read these posts by Baggs and Regan, they chilled me to the bone. Not just because I remembered what had sometimes been done to me, but because I saw for the first time exactly who SGJ was trying to be, and that it was not good to be her. SGJ does not respect my experience or my feelings as an autistic person: when I am being SGJ, I am treating myself as the little girl playing teacher treats the recalcitrant doll she must move around, speak for and chastise. She forces me to do and tolerate things that make me uncomfortable, unhappy and drained, while telling me that she is only acting for my good and for the good of people around me. She tells me that my resistance to her comes from the side of me that must be disavowed, the side that is identified with those 'other' autistics, such as Mel Baggs, whose fate I am privileged, through SGJ's good offices, to escape. SGJ wants me to feel good that I am not Mel Baggs; she wants me to pity and distance myself from them, and other autistic people like them. She wants me to do this even though Baggs's activism has helped me to find myself, and to write these very words. SGJ is the personification of my internalized ableism, and as such she perpetuates harm not only to me, but also to my fellow autistic people who cannot or do not pass as neurotypical, and who do not or cannot let it go when autistic people as a class are harmed or erased or insulted.

She is, moreover, that most nauseating of disabled types, the 'supercrip', this being 'a disparaging term for disabled people who overcompensate for their supposed deficiencies', and 'overcome' their disability to take their place as the centre of an 'inspirational', triumphalist narrative, to show how even naturally unfortunate people might will themselves into being fortunate, if only they'd try.[206]

There's internalized ableism in SGJ, internalized misogyny from taking in judgements about my 'strident' mother and my 'intimidating' self, internalized Anti-Semitism that tells me that Jewish women are 'loud' and 'pushy', and a woman should not be like that. Reading Baggs and Regan made me realize that she was harmful not only to me, but to other autistic women too. Talking to Kate Fox made me realize that she was perpetuating class-bound standards of female behaviour that were designed to mark out 'nice' middle-class girls, who deserved politeness, from 'common' working-class ones, who could be treated rudely. And reading Mona Eltahawy made me realize that she was white to her core, and how insidiously harmful that whiteness can be to women who cannot embody it.

Eltahawy writes about anger, how it is taboo for women, and how some women risk more than others by expressing their anger. As she says, 'depending on their race and class, some girls are punished for behaviour that is tolerated in others'.[207] In 2019, I spent Boxing Day reading Candice Carty-Williams's novel *Queenie*, and I was struck by the number of scenes in which the young black protagonist encounters defensiveness or even outright hostility when white people interpret her expressions of distress as unreasonable or threatening. Observing the shock of white American feminists at the election of Donald Trump in 2016, Eltahawy describes it as the reaction of a protected group who had been able to live in denial about the implacable nature of the patriarchy they lived under and cherish an 'unjustified over-confidence... especially about the achievements of feminism and what it had shielded them from'. That they have been quiescent for so long 'is a reminder of how privileged and sheltered white American women have been from the injustices that ignite rage in Black women and girls, for which they are punished and stereo-typed'. She points out that 'White women have the most privilege of expressing anger and are the last to express it, because they are sheltered from so much that ignites anger in the rest of us.'[208]

I need to have a conversation with SGJ, a difficult one. I need to remind myself that not all difficult conversations can or should be avoided.

You were not one of those women who could hide behind the façade of Socially Gracious Womanhood, and not just because of your temperament. You were a lone female householder and you had to work hard; when you needed help you had to ask for it directly, and sometimes repeatedly; you had to shift, and argue, for yourself. Your directness and lack of womanly softness might have cost you, but you could not have survived all those years without being tough, and showing it. (Neither could my single great-aunt Yetta, her hard-working widowed sister Mary or the widow's daughter, my mother.)

The arguments that your son Johannes made in your defence showed again and again how well he understood this, and it was his defence that saved you. As an intellectually brilliant man, who had been picked out as a boy to receive an excellent education, and who had been shrewd enough to use this education to move up in the world and gain a network of influential friends, he had at his disposal all the resources which your sex had denied you. As a man with a public profile, he was allowed to be all the things that you were not: assertive, persistent, forensic in his dissection of the poor arguments and flawed characters of your accusers.

Undermining the credibility of these witnesses was entirely necessary to build his defence, but it still saddens me to see how one woman's good character was upheld through the public humiliation of another. Ursula Reinbold had never had the most spotless reputation in Leonberg, and the Keplers had made as much as they could of the whispers about her. In January 1617, Christoph and his brother-in-law Georg Binder wrote to the Duke, alleging not only that Reinbold had been seen going about her business in good health, and was therefore demonstrably a liar, but also that she was 'hated by everyone and known as a whore; she had even been imprisoned for illicit sex'.[209] Even if she were ill, it had to be because of her dubious sexual activity, and the 'forbidden "devilish"' medicines she used.

Kepler returned to this theme in his final defence, using his knowledge of medicine to assert that Ursula was deranged, and that this derangement was the result of a sexually transmitted disease. He raked over Ursula's past, turning up dirt from her youth in her hometown. According to Kepler, Ursula had fallen pregnant after a liaison with a local apprentice pharmacist, who had given her the wherewithal to end the pregnancy; it was this, he said, that had made her sterile. You, by contrast, had lived blamelessly as a widow for thirty-two years, and had kept your own daughter's reputation spotless until she was married to her pastor husband. Surely if any woman had the attributes expected of a witch, it was the wicked Ursula Reinbold. It is not easy to feel sorry for Reinbold, who was responsible for inflicting so much harm on you and your family, but when people seek to undermine a woman's credibility by drawing attention to her sexual behaviour, there was, and is, misogyny at work. This still happens to women. It does not happen to men.

However much I might flinch at some of your son's methods, they were, in the end, effective: they freed you from imprisonment, and they helped to save your life. But your own strength and integrity made a difference too. After the Tübingen lawyers considered all the evidence from both sides, they declared that the case against you was insufficient to justify physical torture, but that the case for you was not strong enough for you to be absolved. You were to be led to the executioner, and shown his torture instruments, in a final effort to force you to confess.

On 28 September 1621, you were taken to the town hall, where you held firm. Rublack has taken your words from the scribe's minutes, and rendered them into direct speech. You said: 'I do not want to confess or admit anything at all. Even if you treat me whatever way you want, and tear out one vein after the next out of my body, I would not know what to admit to.'[210] You appealed to God and your faith. You still did not cry, not even when they threatened you, repeatedly, with torture. In the end, they gave up. Six days later, you were freed, and, in early October, absolved.

There's a passage from an article by Nicola Clark, published in the *Guardian* in 2016, that seems to me to go straight to the heart of the matter:

Women are still expected to behave as others dictate, from the function of our uterus, to the way we express ourselves in person or on the page. For women with autism our capacity and interest in conformity is diminished – we are no friend to the patriarchy.[211]

As autistic people, we feel the pull of the truth as we see it more naturally and more powerfully than we feel the pull of fitting in. It is not that we choose to be this way: as Clark says, there is such a thing as a capacity for conformity and ours is relatively weak. You could see this as a disability, a dangerous deficit that nearly got you executed, and you would be right. Although you were freed, you were never able to return to your home in Leonberg, and you died six months later. You could also see it as an advantage that gave you the ability to face the forces of patriarchy down and force them to concede defeat, and in this, you would also be right. Even under threat of torture, you would not swerve from your truth.

I find Clark's distinction between 'capacity' and 'interest' to be crucial here. We have no control over our natural capacity for conformity, but we can make decisions about how interested in conformity we choose to be, and how much we choose to pursue acceptance. I have been aware for all my adult life that I have been making decisions of this kind, and I have always understood them to be personal, a question of how far I want to protect myself and be kind to others around me. But of course, the personal is never only the personal: the personal is political. I'm beginning to think that I chose to push this truth to one side for too long.

Even allowing for my extensive deployment of SGJ, it is still true that in any meeting I am the one most likely to draw attention to the obvious problem that everyone else is studiously not mentioning. Sometimes I don't realize that this is what I've done, until someone comes up to me afterwards and thanks me for being 'brave' and 'outspoken'. Over the last couple of years, I have watched in awe as a younger autistic woman, Greta Thunberg, has drawn attention to the most obvious and serious problem of our time – the ongoing climate disaster. She has been acclaimed for this, but she has also been vilified, and much of the vilification has centred around her lack of normative femininity – her directness, her uncompromising manner of communicating the truth to powerful men without softening the message, her refusal to simper, her unsmiling face. A hundred years ago, Virginia Woolf wrote that men have always used women as mirrors to reflect them back at twice their size. In Greta's eyes, powerful, narcissistic men see themselves as they are, and they do not like it, and they blame her for showing them.

Thunberg's example has made me realize that I have been squashing a part of myself that is not only acceptable, but actually useful, to me and to others. My reading has given me some insight into the forces that have caused me to be afraid of that part of myself, and the consequences of inhabiting it. I've mentioned Sara Ahmed and Mona Eltahawy, Minna Salami and Nicola Clark. Kate Manne has explained very clearly how misogyny arises from gendered expectations about women's behaviour – that we should be accommodating and nurturing towards the men around us, and that when we fail to do so we are depriving them of that to which they are justly entitled.[212] We should listen to them, we should not correct or contradict or interrupt them, we should not – as my mother once caused consternation by doing – refuse to laugh at their sexist jokes. If a woman does not comply, then she is the problem, the 'feminist killjoy', the Old Dragon, the Battleaxe, the Termagant, the Nippy Sweety, the Uppity Cow, the Bitch.

I've come to understand all that, and also to understand that ableism works in the same way, that as an autistic person I am not supposed to make assertions that cause non-autistic people – parents of autistic children, autistic professionals – to feel bad about themselves. If, as an autistic person, I make a non-autistic person feel bad about themselves in relation to autism, it must be because I am a defective person, lacking both an adult understanding of my own condition and empathy for the individuals who are trying so patiently to cope with the consequences of it. I see this very argument – if I must dignify it with that word – used on social media again and again, whenever an autistic person seeks to advocate for autistic people as a group.

In the face of all this, I've shrunk away from speaking up. Too Much. Katharina, I need to speak up more. Maybe I'll start with a letter to that schoolmaster – someone needs to tell him he's a prick.

Yours, in sharp-tongued sisterhood,
Joanne

Afterword

Letter to Caron Freeborn

Oh Caron,

You were so much a part of the process of writing this book – as you were for every one of my books, ever since I met you. I sent you the letter to Virginia for your approval, and the letter to Adelheid, and to Frau V. When I realized I would never get to send you the letter to Katharina, I didn't know what to do with it, or myself. I never thought for a moment that the last letter would be addressed to you.

   You were one of my very closest weird sisters, and one of my closest writing sisters too. My weird writing sister. Today I read your article on the autistic line in poetry.[213] You had, you said, a 'special interest' in the poetic line, in all the ways that a poet might modify it so as 'to play with the tension between the grammar and the line break, and to choose according to internal pressure'. You understood that your writing self was inextricable from your autistic self: you didn't write 'in spite of' your autism, but 'with' your autism. In the biography that follows the article you describe yourself as 'autistic, perseverating on details others discard'. That's as good a definition of autism as I've ever read, and reminds me of the value of the unclassified routes down which our autistic brains so often travel. Speed, familiarity and convenience are good, but they aren't everything. Sometimes you need the difficulty to get where you're going.

You helped me to stay with the difficulty. When I first suspected that I was autistic, you were one of the first people I went to, to see if that suspicion might be confirmed. There was autism in your family, so I felt confident that you would understand both me and autism thoroughly enough to make a sound judgement. At that point, you were writing your novel, *Presenting... The Fabulous O'Learys*,[214] and when I read it, I thought for a moment – wrongly – that you might have based aspects of your autistic character Delia on me. Delia likes to watch coloured stones running through her hands. I told you this reminded me of something, how as a teenager I had a penchant for buying lengths of silk and velvet ribbon from the haberdashery department of the Brent Cross branch of John Lewis. Madonna was in her pomp and lace and ribbons were fashionable, but I didn't put them in my hair. I had thought I meant to wear them, but it turned out that what I really wanted them for was for keeping them rolled up in a desk drawer, so that I could occasionally take them out, unfurl them, and watch them running through my fingers. It was one of those things that had always baffled me about myself – why did I do that? Other people didn't do things like that.

When I told you about the ribbons, you rolled your eyes and said, 'No, *that's* not autistic at all, is it, Joanne?'

I remember that conversation very well. We were sitting in the canteen at the university where you taught Creative Writing and where you insisted, every time, on paying for my lunch. This bothered me, I explained, because I had always thought that a good friendship was symmetrical – for example, you should take turns to initiate contact, and if you didn't it meant something was out of whack. It was only as I was speaking to you that I realized my habit of seeing friendship as a balance sheet was an autistic one, a rule that I used to help me navigate territory that I always found bewildering. I've since learned to ditch that rule, and live, uncomfortably, with the bewilderment. I never know where I am with people; I accept that I never will.

No two autistic people are alike, in their strengths or their weaknesses. You had a better grasp on relationships and how they worked, but you shared my difficulty with literal navigation. We were both place-blind, and the last time I ever performed with you, we began the evening by walking round and round the outside of a pub, failing to find the right entrance. It turned out we'd been following each other's lead – a big mistake on both sides.

You were better at relationships, and much, much better at speaking up when speaking up was needed, so it always struck me as strange that you found it so impossible to promote your work. In your article on the line, you wrote: 'I think it's hard to be an autistic writer as for many of us, we can't easily publicize our work… I am a source of frustration to publishers as I can make any change required without fuss, produce anything they want almost to order, but I don't know how to tell the world I'm here.' I knew that this was something I could help you with, and I told the world you were in it at every opportunity. I taught your work, and not just because I loved you but I knew the work was wonderful. One of the many terrible things about your death is that it put an abrupt end to a period of incredible creativity for you. We all thought – all your many writing friends – that you were writing the poems that would make your name. We'll keep your name out there, Caron Freeborn.

There was, in the end, some symmetry to our relationship: just as you had helped me towards my formal autistic diagnosis, I was, eight years later, able to support you through yours. That confirmation was important to you, and so I'm so glad for you that you got it; I only wish you could have lived with it for longer.

I wish I could have sent the Katharina Kepler letter to you. When I sent you the first draft of the Letter to Adelheid Bloch, you gave it a general thumbs up, but said how infuriated you were by the way I kept stopping to apologize: 'I just kept thinking – stop fucking apologizing, woman!' We'd said – and written, and posted – other words to each other since, but when I heard you'd died, it was those words that came echoing back, first and loudest. I held them in my head as I wrote the Kepler letter, and thought about what it would mean to be an unapologetic sort of woman, the sort you knew how to be. So you were with me for that chapter – not in the way I would have wished you to be, but there all the same.

You're here now. I'm always going to keep you with me as I write, from now on, and I make no fucking apology for that.

Rest defiantly, Caron Freeborn,
    and may your memory be a blessing,
        your weird sister,
           Joanne
           01/06/2020

Appendix

From DisHuman.com[215]

OUR DISHUMAN MANIFESTO

- Unpacks and troubles dominant notions of what it means to be human;
- Celebrates the disruptive potential of disability to trouble these dominant notions;
- Acknowledges that being recognized as a regular normal human being is desirable, especially for those people who have been denied access to the category of the human;
- Recognizes disability's intersectional relationship with other identities that have been considered less than human (associated with class, gender, sexuality, ethnicity, age);
- Aims to develop theory, research, art and activism that push at the boundaries of what it means to be human and disabled;
- Keeps in mind the pernicious and stifling impacts of ableism, which we define as discriminatory processes that idealize a narrow version of humanness and reject more diverse forms of humanity;

- Seeks to promote transdisciplinary forms of empirical and theoretical enquiry that breaks disciplinary orthodoxies, dominances and boundaries;
- Foregrounds dis/ability as the complex for interrogating oppression and furthering a posthuman politics of affirmation.

Selected Further Reading

Ahmed, Sara, *Living a Feminist Life* (Durham, NC: Duke University Press, 2017)

Beardon, Luke, *Autism and Asperger Syndrome in Adults* (London: Sheldon Press, 2017)

Eltahawy, Mona, *The Seven Necessary Sins for Women and Girls* (Boston, MA: Beacon Press, 2019)

Evans, Susanne E., *Forgotten Crimes: The Holocaust and People with Disabilities* (Chicago: Ivan R. Dee, 2004)

Feinstein, Adam, *A History of Autism: Conversations with the Pioneers* (Chichester: Wiley-Blackwell, 2010)

Fernyhough, Charles (ed.), *Others: Writers on the power of words to help us see beyond ourselves* (London: Unbound, 2019)

Goodley, Dan, *Disability Studies: An Interdisciplinary Introduction*, 2nd Edition (London: Sage, 2017)

Grant, Lana, *From Here to Maternity: Pregnancy and Motherhood on the Autism Spectrum* (London and Philadelphia: Jessica Kingsley Publishers, 2015)

Huxley-Jones, Lizzie, *Stim: An Autistic Anthology* (London: Unbound, 2020)

Jack, Jordynn, *Autism and Gender: From Refrigerator Mothers to Computer Geeks* (Urbana, Chicago and Springfield: University of Illinois Press, 2014)

James, Laura, *Odd Girl Out: Being an Autistic Woman in a Neurotypical World* (London: Bluebird, 2018)

Johnson, Kelley and Traustadóttir, Rannveig (eds), *Women with Intellectual Disabilities: Finding a Place in the World* (London: Jessica Kingsley Publishers, 2000)

Kafer, Alison, *Feminist, Queer, Crip* (Bloomington: Indiana University Press, 2013)

Kittay, Eve Feder, *Learning from My Daughter: The Value and Care of Disabled Minds* (Oxford: Oxford University Press, 2019)

Kleege, Georgina, *Blind Rage: Letters to Helen Keller* (Washington DC: Gallaudet University Press, 2006)

Lee, Hermione, *Virginia Woolf* (London: Chatto & Windus, 1996)

Lorde, Audrey, *Sister Outsider: Essays and Speeches* (Berkeley: Crossing Press, 2007)

May, Katherine, *The Electricity of Every Living Thing: One Woman's Walk with Asperger's* (London: Trapeze, 2018)

May, Katherine (ed.), *The Best Most Awful Job: Twenty Writers Talk Honestly About Motherhood* (London: Elliott & Thompson, 2020)

McDonagh, Patrick, *Idiocy: A Cultural History* (Liverpool: Liverpool University Press, 2008)

McGrath, James, *Naming Adult Autism: Culture, Science, Identity* (London: Rowman & Littlefield International, 2017)

Morgen, Laurie, *Travelling by Train: The Journey of an Autistic Mother* (St Albans: Panoma Press, 2020)

Murray, Stuart, *Representing Autism: Culture, Narrative, Fascination* (Liverpool University Press, 2008)

Nadesan, Maija Holmer, *Constructing Autism: Unravelling the 'Truth' and Understanding the Social* (London: Routledge, 2005)

Prahlad, Anand, *The Secret Life of a Black Aspie: A Memoir* (Fairbanks, AK: University of Alaska Press, 2017)

Rublack, Ulinka, *The Astronomer and the Witch: Johannes Kepler's Fight for His Mother* (Oxford: Oxford University Press, 2015)

Ryan, Frances, *Crippled: Austerity and the Demonization of Disabled People*, 2nd Edition (New York: Verso, 2020)

Salami, Minna, *Sensuous Knowledge: A Black Feminist Approach for Everyone* (London: Zed Books, 2020)

Salman, Saba (ed.), *Made Possible: Stories of success by people with learning disabilities – in their own words* (London: Unbound, 2020)

Sequenzia, Amy and Grace, Elizabeth J. (eds), *Typed Words, Loud Voices* (Fort Worth: Autonomous Press, 2015)

Sheffer, Edith, *Asperger's Children: The Origins of Autism in Nazi Vienna* (New York: W. W. Norton, 2018)

Silberman, Steve, *NeuroTribes: The Legacy of Autism and How to Think Smarter About People Who Think Differently* (London: Allen & Unwin, 2015)

Woolf, Virginia, *A Room of One's Own* and *Three Guineas* (London: Vintage, 1996)

Yergeau, Melanie, *Authoring Autism: On Rhetoric and Neurological Queerness* (Durham, NC: Duke University Press, 2017)

Blogs and websites

Cal Montgomery, https://montgomerycal.wordpress.com/

Kerima Çevik, https://theautismwars.blogspot.com/

Mel Baggs, https://ballastexistenz.wordpress.com/about-2/

Mel Baggs, https://cussinanddiscussin.wordpress.com/author/ameliabaggs/

Morénike Giwa Onaiwu, https://morenikego.com/

Autistic Women and Nonbinary Network, https://awnnetwork.org/
Scottish Women's Autism Network, https://swanscotland.org/
Watch Mel Baggs's film, *In My Language*, here: https://www.
youtube.com/watch?v=JnylM1hI2jc
Watch Kenny Fries's series of films about T4, *What Happened Here in the Summer of 1940?*, here: https://www.kennyfries.com/summer-of-1940

Acknowledgements

I would like to thank, as always, my agent Louise Greenberg, Karen Duffy, Clare Drysdale and all at Atlantic Books, Tamsin Shelton for her brilliant copy-editing, and my husband, Chris Hadley. Huge thanks are also due to friends and family who read and commented on the chapters as I wrote them: Richard Ashcroft, Kaddy Benyon, Lisa Gee, Caron Freeborn and Priya Khanchandani. I would also like to thank Arifa Akbar, Emily Berry, Charles Fernyhough, Katherine May and Eva Wiseman, for commissioning essays and articles in which I could explore my ideas about autistic, female identity. Thanks are due to Nicky Clark and Dr Jo Edge, Lutz Kaelber and Dr Frank Janzowski for answering questions. Finally, I would like to express my gratitude to Ivanova Smith, Melanie Mahjenta and Freyja Haraldsdóttir for permitting me to use the stuff of their lives, and to those who gave their approval on behalf of those who were no longer here: Mel Baggs' close friend Anne Corwin, Caron's partner Chris Baines and the family of Adelheid Bloch.

Thanks and love are also due to my autistic writing sisters, Kate Fox, Laura James, Katherine May (once more) and Rhi Lloyd-Williams, for sharing experience, and also to James McGrath, for helping me to understand why I'm doing the work that I'm doing. And to Las Autistas, who know who they are.

A Note on Permissions

The author and publisher wish to thank the following for permission to quote from copyright material:

Material from Patience Agbabi's article 'My son was diagnosed with autism at five. Did he inherit it from my misunderstood mother?' theguardian.com, 28.3.2020 reproduced by permission of Guardian News & Media Ltd. Quotations from Hannah Gadsby's New York Times interview are reprinted by permission of Hannah Gadsby; material from Virginia Woolf's diaries, reprinted by permission of The Society of Authors as the Literary Representative of the Estate of Virginia Woolf; excerpt from *Carrie* copyright © 1974 by Stephen King, reprinted by permission of Hodder & Stoughton, An Hachette UK Company; excerpt from *On Writing: A Memoir of the Craft* copyright © 2000 by Stephen King, reprinted by permission of Hodder & Stoughton, An Hachette UK Company; *Beginning Again: An Autobiography of the Years 1911-1918* reprinted by permission of The University of Sussex and The Society of Authors as the Literary Representative of the Estate of Leonard Woolf; material from Frances Ryan's *Crippled: Austerity and the Demonization of Disabled People* reprinted by permission of Verso Books; material from *Idiocy: A Cultural History* by Patrick McDonagh © by Patrick McDonagh 2008, Liverpool University Press, reproduced with permission of the Licensor through PLSClear; material from

Every effort has been made to trace or contact all copyright-holders. The publishers will be pleased to make good any omissions or rectify any mistakes brought to their attention at the earliest opportunity.

Notes

Foreword: Letter to the Reader

1 Sigmund Freud, 'The "Uncanny"' [1919] in Anna Freud, James Strachey, Alix Strachey and Alan Tyson (eds), *The Standard Edition of the Complete Psychological Works of Sigmund Freud, Vol XVII (1917–1919)* (London: Vintage, 2001).

2 Audre Lorde, *Sister Outsider: Essays and Speeches by Audre Lorde* (Berkeley: Crossing Press, 2007).

3 Sara Ahmed, *Living a Feminist Life* (Durham: Duke University Press, 2017).

4 Kimberle Crenshaw, 'Demarginalizing the Intersection of Race and Sex: A Black Feminist Critique of Antidiscrimination Doctrine, Feminist Theory and Antiracist Politics' in Joy James and T. Denean Sharpley-Whiting (eds), *The Black Feminist Reader* (Oxford: Blackwell Publishers, 2000).

5 Steve Silberman, *NeuroTribes: The Legacy of Autism and How to Think Smarter About People Who Think Differently* (London: Allen & Unwin, 2015).

6 David Marchese, 'Hannah Gadsby on comedy trolls, anti-vaxxers and burying her dog', *New York Times*, 25 May 2020, https://www.nytimes.com/interactive/2020/05/25/magazine/hannah-gadsby-interview.html

7 Daniel Goodley and Katherine Runswick-Cole, 'Becoming dishuman: thinking about the human through dis/ability', *Discourse: Studies in the Cultural Politics of Education*, Vol. 37, Issue 1, 2016.

8 Edith Sheffer, *Asperger's Children: The Origins of Autism in Nazi Vienna* (New York: W. W. Norton, 2018).

9 Ulinka Rublack, *The Astronomer and the Witch: Johannes Kepler's Fight for His Mother* (Oxford: Oxford University Press, 2015).
10 Patience Agbabi, 'My son was diagnosed with autism at five. Did he inherit it from my misunderstood mother?', *Guardian*, 28 March 2020, https://www.theguardian.com/lifeandstyle/2020/mar/28/autism-son-diagnosed-at-five-did-he-inherit-it-from-my-mother
11 See Sara Ahmed's blog, https://feministkilljoys.com/
12 Georgina Kleege, *Blind Rage: Letters to Helen Keller* (Washington DC: Gallaudet University Press, 2006)

Letter to Virginia Woolf

13 Virginia Woolf, *A Room of One's Own* and *Three Guineas* (London: Vintage, 1996), pp. 70–71.
14 Virginia Woolf, *Moments of Being: Unpublished Autobiographical Writings*, ed. Jeanne Schulkind (New York and London: Harcourt Brace Jovanovich, 1976), p. 130.
15 Stephen King, *Carrie* (London: Hodder, 2011), p. 6.
16 Ibid., p. 3.
17 Ibid., p. 6.
18 Ibid., pp. xv–xvi.
19 Stephen King, *On Writing: A Memoir of the Craft* (London: Hodder, 2012), p. 87.
20 Originally published in *Ms.* Magazine. Ellen Cronan Rose (ed.), *Critical Essays on Margaret Drabble* (Boston: G. K. Hall, 1985).
21 Margaret Drabble, *A Summer Bird-Cage* (Harmondsworth: Penguin Books, 1985), p. 13.
22 Ibid.
23 Ibid., pp. 20–21.
24 Ibid., p. 110.
25 Ibid., p. 113.
26 Ibid., p. 114.
27 Ibid., p. 110.
28 Ibid., pp. 31–2.
29 Ibid., p. 31.

30 https://www.theguardian.com/books/interactive/2013/may/18/
margaret-drabble-summer-birdcage-annotations
31 Ellen Z. Lambert, 'Margaret Drabble and the sense of possibility'
in Cronan Rose (ed.), pp. 36–7.
32 Anne Olivier Bell (ed.), *The Diary of Virginia Woolf, Vol.1, 1915–19*
(London: Hogarth Press, 1977), entry for 15 February 1915.
33 Virginia Woolf, *Mrs Dalloway* (London: Penguin Popular Classics,
1996), p. 14.
34 Ibid., pp.14–15.
35 Quoted in Hermione Lee, *Virginia Woolf* (London: Chatto &
Windus, 1996), p. 390.
36 Anne Olivier Bell (ed.), *The Diary of Virginia Woolf, Vol. 3, 1925–
1930* (London: Hogarth Press, 1980), entry for 21 December 1925.
37 Letter to Harold Nicolson, 19 December 1922, https://www.
brainpickings.org/2016/07/28/virginia-woolf-vita-sackville-west/
38 Woolf, *Mrs Dalloway*, p. 143.
39 Leonard Woolf, *Beginning Again: An Autobiography of the Years
1911–1918* (London: Hogarth Press, 1964), p. 29.
40 Iris Marion Young, 'Throwing Like a Girl: A Phenomenology of
Feminine Body Comportment Motility and Spatiality', *Human
Studies*, Vol. 3, No. 2 (April 1980), pp. 137–56 .
41 Woolf, *Mrs Dalloway*, pp. 141–2.
42 Virginia Woolf, *Jacob's Room* (New York: Harcourt, Brace and Co.,
1923), p. 82.
43 Quoted in Paul John Eakin, *The Ethics of Life Writing* (Ithaca and
London: Cornell University Press, 2004), p. 8.
44 Woolf, *A Room of One's Own*, p. 33.
45 Ibid.
46 Woolf, *Mrs Dalloway*, p. 100.
47 Ibid., p. 101.
48 Ibid., p. 110.
49 Woolf, *Moments of Being*, p. 151.
50 Ibid., p. 152.
51 Ibid., p. 129.
52 Ibid.

Letter to Adelheid Bloch

53 Lutz Kaelber, 'Jewish Children with Disabilities and Nazi "Euthanasia" Crimes', *The Bulletin of the Carolyn and Leonard Miller Center for Holocaust Studies*, Vol. 17, Spring 2013, p. 17.
54 Ibid.
55 Daniel McConnell, 'Autism and Neurodiversity: A Panel Presentation at the 2008 Autism National Committee Conference' in Amy Sequenzia and Elizabeth J. Grace (eds), *Typed Words, Loud Voices* (Fort Worth: Autonomous Press, 2015), p. 49.
56 Franz Peschke, 'Economics, Murder and Planned Economy: The Wiesloch Medical and Nursing Home in the Third Reich' in *Aspects of Medical Philosophy*, Volume 10, 2012
57 https://www.collinsdictionary.com/dictionary/english/idiot
58 Patrick McDonagh, *Idiocy: A Cultural History* (Liverpool: Liverpool University Press, 2008).
59 A. Fitzherbert, *Nouvelle Natura Brevium* (London: 1553), quoted in Richard Neugebauer, 'Mental handicap in medieval and early modern England: Criteria, measurement and care' in A. Digby and W. Wright (eds), *From Idiocy to Mental Deficiency: Historical Perspectives on People with Learning Disabilities* (London and New York: Routledge, 1996).
60 John Rastell, *Exposition of Certaine Difficulte and Obscure Words and Termes* (1527), quoted in McDonagh, p. 86.
61 Sheffer, p. 64.
62 Frances Ryan, *Crippled: Austerity and the Demonization of Disabled People* (New York: Verso, 2020), p. 41.
63 Mel Baggs, 'Losing' in Steven K. Kapp (ed.), *Autistic Community and the Neurodiversity Movement: Stories from the Frontline* (London: Palgrave Macmillan, 2020), p. 77.
64 *Panorama's Undercover Care: The Abuse Exposed* was broadcast on BBC One on Tuesday 31 May 2011.
65 King James Version.
66 C. F. Goodey, 'John Locke's idiots in the natural history of mind', *History of Psychiatry*, v (1994), p. 217.

67 'Essay Concerning Human Understanding', II.11.20, quoted in Goodey, p. 217.
68 Goodey, p. 218.
69 'Essay Concerning Human Understanding', III.6.21–22, quoted in Goodey, p. 229.
70 Goodey, p. 227.
71 McDonagh, p. 65.
72 Quoted in ibid., p. 67.
73 Lennard J. Davis, 'Introduction: Disability, Normality and Power' in Lennard J. Davis (ed.), *The Disability Studies Reader* (London: Routledge, 2017), p. 2.
74 https://mn.gov/mnddc/parallels/four/4a/2.html#:~:text=Esquirol%20 divided%20intellectual%20deficiency%20into,their%20 organization%20is%20nearly%20normal.&text=Esquirol%20 defined%20%22idiots%22%20as%20persons,idiots%20 cannot%20control%20their%20senses
75 https://wellcomecollection.org/works/nm2y6bkr/download? sierraId=b21360881, pp. 4–5.
76 Stephen Jay Gould, *The Mismeasure of Man* (London: Penguin Books, 1996), p. 179.
77 Kelley Johnson and Rannveig Traustadóttir (eds), *Women with Intellectual Disabilities: Finding a Place in the World* (London and Philadelphia: Jessica Kingsley Publishers, 2000), p. 10.
78 Jen Slater, Embla Ágústsdóttir and Freyja Haraldsdóttir, 'Becoming intelligible woman: Gender, disability and resistance at the border zone of youth' in *Feminism and Psychology*, Vol. 28, Issue 3, 2018, p. 411.
79 Tom Batchelor, 'Woman with mental age of child can give birth after court-ordered abortion is overturned', *Independent*, 25 June 2019.
80 Laura Ivanova Smith, 'Mental Age Theory Hurts People with Intellectual Disabilities', 7 September 2017, http://nosmag.org/ mental-age-theory-hurts-people-with-intellectual-disabilities
81 Lewis M. Terman, 'The Intelligence Quotient of Francis Galton in Childhood', *The American Journal of Psychology*, Vol. 28, No. 2, April 1917, p. 213.

82 Francis Galton, *Inquiries into Human Faculty and Its Development* (London: Macmillan, 1883), p. 24.
83 https://wellcomecollection.org/works/nm2y6bkr/download?sierraId=b21360881, p. 5.
84 Henry Herbert Goddard, *The Kallikak Family: A Study in the Heredity of Feeble-mindedness* (New York: The Macmillan Company, 1913), pp. 101–2.
85 Ibid., p. 101.
86 Ibid.
87 Ibid., pp. 7–8.
88 Ibid., p. 18.
89 Ibid., pp. 18–19.
90 J. David Smith and Michael L. Wehmeyer, 'Who was Deborah Kallikak?', *Journal of Intellectual & Developmental Disability*, 50(2), April 2012, pp. 169–78, NIH Public Access Site, p. 6.
91 Ibid., p. 9.
92 Ibid., p. 10.
93 Olivier Bell (ed.), *The Diary of Virginia Woolf, Vol. 1, 1915–19*, p. 13.
94 https://stolpersteine-konstanz.de/bloch_adelheid.html

Letter to Frau V

95 Hans Asperger, '"Autistic Psychopathy" in Childhood,' in Uta Frith (ed.), *Autism and Asperger Syndrome* (Cambridge: Cambridge University Press, 1991), p. 40.
96 Ibid., p. 41.
97 Ibid.
98 For an account of Zak's work, and much else in this letter, see Sheffer.
99 Quoted in Sheffer, p. 51.
100 Ibid., p. 52.
101 Asperger in Frith (ed.), p. 41.
102 Ibid.
103 Ibid.
104 Ibid., p. 84.

105 The question of Asperger's complicity in the Nazi eugenicist killing programme is a complex and controversial one, which I can't explore in any detail here.

106 Asperger in Frith (ed.), p. 84.

107 One such girl was Adelheid Bloch.

108 Asperger in Frith (ed.), p. 84.

109 Ibid., pp. 50–51.

110 Sheffer, p. 144.

111 Asperger in Frith (ed.), p. 59.

112 Sheffer, p. 165.

113 Ibid.

114 https://www.webmd.com/mental-health/qa/what-is-psychodynamic-therapy

115 Leo Kanner, 'Problems of Nosology and Psychodynamics of Early Infantile Autism', *The American Journal of Orthopsychiatry,* 19(3), 1949, p. 420.

116 Kanner, p. 421.

117 Ibid.

118 Ibid., p. 422.

119 Ibid.

120 Ibid., p. 423.

121 Ibid., p. 424.

122 Ibid., p. 423.

123 Ibid., p. 425.

124 Asperger in Frith (ed.), p. 41.

125 Kanner, p. 423.

126 Ibid.

127 What used to be called 'Munchausen's by Proxy'.

128 A. L. Pohl, S. K. Crockford, C. Allison and S. Baron-Cohen, 'Positive and Negative Experiences of Mothers with Autism', 2016 International Meeting for Autism Research.

129 Amelia Hill, 'Mothers with autism: "I mothered my children in a very different way"', *Guardian*, 15 April 2017, https://www.theguardian.com/lifeandstyle/2017/apr/15/women-autistic-mothers-undiagnosed-children

130 A. L. Pohl, S. K. Crockford, M. Blakemore et al., 'A comparative

study of autistic and non-autistic women's experience of motherhood', *Molecular Autism*, 11, 3, 2020, p. 7.

131 Letter to the Editors entitled 'Crohn's Disease and Asperger Syndrome: Not Just A Coincidence?' in *Inflammatory Bowel Diseases*, Vol. 22, No. 6, June 2016, written by Maria Fragaki, Konstantinos Karmiris and Gregorios Paspatis of General Hospital of Heraklion 'Venizeleio and Pananio'.

132 Pohl, Crockford, Blakemore et al., p. 7.

133 See Adam Feinstein, *A History of Autism: Conversations with the Pioneers* (Chichester: Wiley-Blackwell, 2010), pp. 57–8.

134 Bruno Bettelheim, *The Empty Fortress: Infantile Autism and the Birth of the Self* (New York and London: The Free Press/Collier-Macmillan Limited, 1967), p. 57.

135 Ibid., p. 66.

136 Ibid., p. 7.

137 Feinstein, p. 56.

138 Bettelheim, p. 7.

139 Ibid., p. 66.

140 Ibid., p. 72.

141 Ibid., p. 17.

142 Ibid., p. 23.

143 Feinstein, p. 60.

144 Quoted in Eva Feder Kittay, *Learning from My Daughter: The Value and Care of Disabled Minds* (Oxford: Oxford University Press, 2019), p. 28.

145 Carol Thomas, *Female Forms: Experiencing and Understanding Disability* (Buckingham: Open University Press, 1999).

146 Bernard Rimland, *Infantile Autism: The Syndrome and Its Implications for a Neural Theory of Behavior* (New York: Appleton-Century-Crofts, 1964).

147 Maggi Golding and Jill Stacey (eds), *Autism Mothers Speak Out: Stories of Advocacy and Activism from Around the World* (London: Jessica Kingsley Publishers, 2018).

148 Jordynn Jack, *Autism and Gender: From Refrigerator Mothers to Computer Geeks* (Urbana, Chicago and Springfield: University of Illinois Press, 2014).

149 Amy C. Sousa, 'From Refrigerator Mothers to Warrior-Heroes: The Cultural Identity Transformation of Mothers Raising Children with Intellectual Disabilities', *Symbolic Interaction*, 43:2, Spring 2011, pp. 220–43. The title conflates autism and intellectual disabilities. This is unfortunate but not unusual.

150 Ibid., p. 220.

151 Katherine Runswick-Cole and Sara Ryan, 'Liminal still? Unmothering disabled children', *Disability & Society*, 34:7–8, 2019, p. 1129.

152 Ibid., p. 1131.

153 http://theconversation.com/what-exactly-is-neoliberalism-84755

154 Sarah L. Holloway and Helena Pimlott-Wilson, 'New economy, neoliberal state and professionalised parenting: mother's labour market engagement and state support for social reproduction in class-differentiated Britain', *Transactions of the Institute of British Geographers*, 2016, p. 377.

155 Ibid., p. 378.

156 Runswick-Cole and Ryan, p. 1134.

157 Ibid.

158 Ibid.

159 Ibid., p. 1133.

160 Katherine Runswick-Cole and Daniel Goodley, 'Disability, austerity and cruel optimism in Big Society: Resistance and "The Disability Commons"', *Canadian Journal of Disability Studies*, 4.2, May 2015, p. 179.

161 Virginia Held, *The Ethics of Care: Personal, Political and Global* (Oxford: Oxford University Press, 2006).

162 Goodley and Runswick-Cole, 'Becoming dishuman: thinking about the human through dis/ability'.

163 Aminatta Forna, *The Mother of All Myths: How Society Moulds and Constrains Mothers* (London: HarperCollins, 1999).

164 Katharina Kepler
For details of Katharina's life, world and trial, I have relied on Ulinka Rublack's account in *The Astronomer and the Witch: Johannes Kepler's Fight for His Mother*.

Letter to Katharina Kepler

165 Rublack, p. xxviii.
166 Ronald Hutton, *The Witch: A History of Fear, from Ancient Times to the Present* (New Haven: Yale University Press, 2017).
167 Rublack, p. 126.
168 Ibid., p. 175.
169 Ibid., p. 166.
170 Ibid., p. 76.
171 Ibid., p. 81.
172 Ibid.
173 Mona Eltahawy, *The Seven Necessary Sins for Women and Girls* (Boston: Beacon Press, 2019).
174 Sara Ahmed, 'Feminist Complaint', feministkilljoys blog, 5 December 2014, https://feministkilljoys.com/2014/12/05/complaint/
175 Ibid.
176 Rublack, p. 113.
177 Ibid., p. 219.
178 Alison Phipps, *Me, Not You: The Trouble with Mainstream Feminism* (Manchester: Manchester University Press, 2020).
179 Rublack, p. 219.
180 Ibid., p. 220.
181 Ibid., p. 219.
182 Ibid., p. 217.
183 Gordon Gates, *Trauma, Stigma, and Autism: Developing Resilience and Loosening the Grip of Shame* (London and Philadelphia: Jessica Kingsley Publishers, 2019).
184 Juliet Mitchell, 'Trauma, Recognition, and the Place of Language', *diacritics*, 28.4, Winter 1998, pp. 121–33.
185 Judith Lewis Herman, *Trauma and Recovery: The Aftermath of Violence – From Domestic Abuse to Political Terror* (London: Pandora, 2001), p. 34.
186 Ibid.
187 Ibid.

188 Gates, p. 16.

189 Ibid., p. 65.

190 Ibid., p. 16.

191 Pete Walker, *Complex PTSD: From Surviving to Thriving: A Guide and Map for Recovering from Childhood Trauma* (Lafayette: Azure Coyote, 2013), p. 12.

192 Ibid., p. 228.

193 Rublack, p. 201.

194 Quoted in ibid., p. 202.

195 Ibid., p. 203.

196 Ibid., p. 209.

197 Ibid., p. 210.

198 Ibid.

199 Anna Freud, 'Die Identifizierung mit dem Angreifer' in *Das Ich und die Abwehrmechanismen* (Vienna: Internationaler Psychoanalytischer Verlag, 1936).

200 Minna Salami, *Sensuous Knowledge: A Black Feminist Approach for Everyone* (London: Zed Books, 2020), p. 49.

201 Ibid., p. 50.

202 Ibid., p. 52.

203 Ibid., p. 54.

204 Mel Baggs, 'Nice Lady Therapists and their war against human emotion: class, disability, and culture', Cussin' and Discussin' blog, 4 May 2018, https://cussinanddiscussin.wordpress.com/?s=nice+lady+therapists

205 Ruti Regan, 'Nice Lady Therapists', Real Social Skills blog, 6 August 2014.

206 G. Thomas Couser, 'Signifying Selves: Disability and Life Writing' in Clare Barker and Stuart Murray (eds), *The Cambridge Companion to Literature and Disability* (Cambridge: Cambridge University Press, 2017), p. 203.

207 Eltahawy, p. 8.

208 Ibid., p. 34.

209 Rublack, p. 117.

210 Ibid., p. 266.

211 Nicola Clark, 'I was diagnosed with autism in my 40s. It's not

just a male condition', *Guardian*, 30 August 2016, https://www.theguardian.com/commentisfree/2016/aug/30/diagnosed-autism-male-condition-women-misdiagnosed

212 Kate Manne, *Down Girl: The Logic of Misogyny* (London: Penguin Random House, 2018).

Afterword: Letter to Caron Freeborn

213 Caron Freeborn, 'The Autistic Line', 4 September 2019, https://impspired.com/2019/09/04/caron-freeborn/

214 Caron Freeborn, *Presenting... The Fabulous O'Learys* (Newbury: Holland House, 2017).

Appendix

215 https://disabilityuos.wordpress.com/dishuman-com/